# NEGOTIATING SCIENCE

# NEGOTIATING SCIENCE

The Critical Role

of Argument in

Student Inquiry

**Brian Hand • Lori Norton-Meier • Jay Staker • Jody Bintz**
FOREWORD BY WENDY SAUL

x

HEINEMANN
PORTSMOUTH, NH

**Heinemann**
361 Hanover Street
Portsmouth, NH 03801–3912
www.heinemann.com

*Offices and agents throughout the world*

**Library of Congress Cataloging-in-Publication Data**
Negotiating science : the critical role of argument in student inquiry,
     grades 5–10  / Brian Hand . . . [et al.].
          p. cm.
     Includes bibliographical references and index.
     ISBN-13: 978-0-325-02607-7
     ISBN-10: 0-325-02607-6
     1. Science—Study and teaching (Middle school).   2. Science—Study and
teaching (Secondary).    3. Inquiry-based learning.   I. Hand, Brian.
Q181.N395 2009
507.1'2—dc22                                                          2008044972

*Editor:* Robin Najar
*Production:* Lynne Costa
*Cover design:* Jenny Jensen Greenleaf
*Cover photograph:* Kim Wise
*Typesetter:* Publishers' Design and Production Services, Inc.
*Manufacturing:* Steve Bernier

Printed in the United States of America on acid-free paper
12   11   10   09   08      VP      1   2   3   4   5

This book is dedicated to the teachers and students who were willing to give the SWH approach a go.

# Contents

# Foreword

How can students' work in literacy support their understanding of science? How can their work in science actually improve literacy skills? These two questions serve as bookends for educators seeking to build curricula—curricula that is intellectually rich, that invites work from students with various abilities and interests, and that enables teachers to do "more than one thing at a time." While others have sought to build and provide advice on using content-rich reading materials, the authors of *Negotiating Science: The Critical Role of Argument in Student Inquiry, Grades 5–10* have instead—and perhaps more effectively—exploited the deep connections between science and writing. For those who value inquiry, these are arguably the most robust and easiest connections to mine, for both teachers and students.

Inquiry, ultimately, is about finding thoughtful answers to questions that matter. In this book—chock-full of sage advice and real examples—teachers learn how to scaffold inquiry. This is not, however, a step-by-step scripted program. Rather, the authors are clear in their commitment to "teaching in the service of learning." What this means in practical terms is that teachers become more adept at listening carefully to students, interacting with them as they interpret puzzling scientific events, encouraging conversation and written documentation of what has happened, and, most important, helping them identify their claims and evidence. Perhaps more than teaching in the service of learning, this programs supports teaching in the service of understanding.

A few key ideas continue to impress me as I work with SWH (Science Writing Heuristic) methods and strategies. First, as the authors insist, I am increasingly convinced that curiosity is essential but not enough—that it is the job of the school to help situate curiosity in what are called the "big ideas" of science. In this sense, it is the teacher's job to tie the curriculum to curiosity-producing hands-on activities, and tie hands-on activities to the communication of those big ideas. This matrix—

the curricular ties, the hands-on investigations, and the assessment of student understanding—is realized through student explanation.

Reading-based approaches often begin by forefronting the big ideas of science with chapter previews and a study guide, in a sense making science appear to be a recitation of big ideas. By contrast, in this book Hand, Norton-Meier, Staker, and Bintz begin by challenging students and engaging them in finding out how things work and what works most reliably and best. Once these students are fully engaged in the doing of science, once they have identified questions of interest and import, other literacy opportunities are introduced, from reading books to a variety of summary-producing activities, from writing letters to creating authentic texts that explain in the students' own words and with their own examples what they have learned.

Those of us in the writing community often talk about "learning to write" as distinct from "writing to learn." The program described here in fact includes both. In the early stages of the process, writing is used as a way to keep track of ideas, notes, and other forms of documentation to help learners rethink and revise their claims. This is what we call writing to learn, that is, using writing as a way to track ideas and make them explicit, to sort out confusions, and to identify contradictions.

In the writing-to-learn phase of the program students use what they have learned to create a variety of genre-based pieces—from stories to descriptions. In so doing they begin to think about their audience, the level of detail, and the kind of examples a reader might need in order to understand a concept. Interestingly, while writing for a reader with less science experience, our student/scientist/author becomes an expert of sorts and takes on the responsibility of presenting clear ideas in a cogent format.

In this sense as students "write in order to learn" they are, in effect, scaffolding their own understanding and allowing their teachers to check in on their metacognitive processes. And when they develop written documents to be shared in some more public forum, they are offering a demonstration of their summative understanding. Of course, from a teacher's perspective this offers educators a double benefit: first, the opportunity to assess student thinking *in situ* as they write to learn, and second, performance-based assignments that can be used for assigning grades.

So let's return to our two overarching goals—to find ways that literacy can support students' understanding of science and ways science can actually improve literacy skills. I think we have both in the SWH program. Literacy is used here to enable the doing of science. As students identify questions and posit claims, they are deeply engaged in the authentic processes of meaning making as practiced by those seeking to better understand the physical world. The writing—and later, the reading about the topic they have chosen to explore—functions somewhat like the crumbs Hansel and Gretel left in order to find their way out of the woods; that is, they provide a record of thinking. Thus, when confused, SWH writing offers students a way to go back when something no longer makes sense or they have lost their intellectual bearings. This is precisely what real scientists do. They make claims and seek evidence to support those claims—and they track those claims and that evidence. But when evidence is not apparent, good scientists need to go back and begin again or pick up from the place that last made sense. It is the writing that allows them to do this.

There is, happily, the added benefit here that actually improves students' literacy skills. It is through the critical thinking that is triggered and practiced in learning science that students ultimately learn to write and read expository text. Knowing from the inside out, as a writer as well as a reader, how argument—that is, claims and evidence—works is a literacy skill now universally recognized as essential. This is the goal of real reading, writing, and speaking and, finally, the gift of real science. I am grateful to the authors of this volume for making these gifts available to science and literacy teachers, but most important, to all of our students.

—*Wendy Saul*

# Acknowledgments

I t seems only appropriate when writing a book about the Science Writing Heuristic approach that we should use the very template that we advocate for science inquiries to express our gratitude to the many people who made this book possible (see the SWH poster inside the front cover). It all started with a question.

1. *Beginning ideas:* We had a question: "How does the SWH approach work in the classroom?" To answer this question, we had the help of many school districts, teachers, students, and administrators who joined us in this inquiry, asked their own questions about science and literacy, and pushed us every day to think deeply about teaching and learning.

2. *Tests:* The test was to examine the use of the SWH approach with classroom teachers in grades 5 through 10. This work would not have been possible without the support of a Math-Science Partnership grant and the State of Iowa, which supported the teachers and researchers to engage in this investigation.

3. *Observations:* We observed, interviewed, videotaped, analyzed, and took notes. We had dialogue and examined our data that led to new observations with an amazing research team including Murat Gunel, Recai Akkus, Sara Nelson, Sarah Trosper, Kyle Rasmussen, Elham Mohammad, Ryan Kelly, Ahmad Al-Kofahi, Migyu Kang, and Bill Crandall. Over the years we have had numerous undergraduate students who have provided support to this project—managing data, scoring writing samples, transcribing, and analyzing: Micale Coon, Jessica Drey, Alicia Johnson, Kevin Jolly, Lori McAlpin, Katie Raymon, Lisa Ryherd, Katherine Schnoor, Sara Ann Smith, and Ashley Titman. In addition, many preservice teachers participated in this project by providing an audience for SWH classrooms through reading and responding to student letters. Your thoughtful responses over the years has made writing purposeful for students. Finally, a special thank-you

goes to the many freshman honors mentees who chose to participate in the project as beginning researchers; your insight has been invaluable.

4. *Claims:* We made claims based on the evidence. Having the opportunity to "go public" with your claims and thinking is a key part of the learning process. Daily, we share our thinking with our colleagues, students, teachers, and friends at Iowa State University and the University of Iowa. We thank you all for your continued support of our questions as teachers, researchers, and writers.

5. *Evidence:* Once the evidence was gathered, we reflected upon our understanding by writing. The results were overwhelming—when teachers are willing to re-examine their beliefs about teaching and learning and give the process a go, both students and teachers are successful. Here we must acknowledge the support of sixty teachers across the United States who read the first draft of this book, "had a go" in their own classrooms, and gave us extensive feedback to bring this revised draft to you. The field testing of the first draft was supported through a Teacher Professional Continuum grant (No. ESI–0537035) through the National Science Foundation. An advisory board, including Donna Alvermann, Sharon Dowd-Jasa, Todd Goodson, Kathy McKee, Wendy Saul, and Larry Yore, has also provided thoughtful response and feedback on our efforts. We thank you for your wisdom and continued "nudging" as we grow in our own understanding of teaching and learning, science and literacy.

6. *Reading:* We asked the experts—of course, the teachers and the students whose stories you will read in this book, but a special thank-you to Jody Beimer, Nate Heying, Lynn Hockenberry, Mark McDermott, Jim Paulson, and Kim Wise who read very early drafts of this book and provided insightful feedback about audience and style.

7. *Reflection:* Finally, reflection. In reflecting on what has made this project possible, we must thank our program assistants, Tracie Miller, Vicki Speake, and Allison Donaldson. Your attention to detail, pep talks, humor, and ability to multitask has made this book an intriguing endeavor and you all reminded us daily of the important work we were doing. Also, a special thank-you to the Heinemann Team and Robin Najar for seeing the value in this project and providing ongoing questions to fuel the writing (and future investigations!).

And, with extreme gratitude and pride, we thank our families who create spaces and time for us to practice what we teach and continually encourage us to "have a go" with our many questions, ideas, and projects about teaching and learning.

# An Introduction

## It's All About Learning

If you are reading this, it is probably a safe guess that you are a teacher who is interested in improving your teaching. This book will take you through a process that you may find mildly shocking that isn't about teaching. The book is more accurately about learning and consequently about how your teaching should be driven by your students' learning. The big idea of what follows is that teaching is in the service of learning. This may seem like a word game but as you work through the book you will find the text continually challenging you on how you view learning and teaching. It is all about learning.

## Examining a New Approach

In this book, you will be introduced to an approach to teaching called the SWH, which stands for the *Science Writing Heuristic*. The word *heuristic* has led to many interesting conversations with researchers, teachers, and students. In language and literacy circles (Halliday, 1975; Smith, 1977; Pinnell, 1985), the term *heuristic* is used to describe language used "to question" or "to wonder." In cognitive theory, a heuristic becomes a template for thinking (Gowin, 1981). For years, we have been asked to change the name, but we find the title indicates to teachers and students that our focus will be on thinking and engaging in intellectually challenging endeavors.

The SWH is a classroom approach that incorporates much more than science inquiry. The approach includes literacy and numeracy in a science context. If you are administrator you will want to take notice as the SWH approach can help both teachers and administrators solve the problem of scheduling. Often schools don't have the time to really focus on science or other topics. The SWH approach creates a seamless flow across literacy, numeracy, and science. As secondary teachers in grades

5 through 10, this may not seem to be an issue but the ever-increasing demand placed on the school schedule is pressuring every segment of curriculum, and every opportunity to streamline helps. The additional benefit this holistic approach produces is an increased sense of learning being an integrated process.

## Teachers as Learners

As you enter into this personal development process, keep in mind some important considerations. This book is the result of years of conversation. The team involved has been discussing, arguing, and challenging each other's thinking for many years. This conversation has taken place in classrooms, teacher workshops, and over lunch, and, in fact, goes on wherever and whenever two or more of us get together. Through these conversations, each team member's understanding of the SWH approach has grown and subsequently become more focused on improving the learning opportunities for our students.

The comments made by the teachers who piloted this book indicated a pattern of interaction with the text that mimicked the conversations that have taken place within the writing team. As the teachers read the book they reacted in the margins with their thoughts, questions, feelings, issues, and arguments. Their approach to reading the book naturally aligned with the SWH approach and demonstrated their own learning processes as they came to a negotiated understanding with the text they were reading and what they were putting into practice in their own classrooms. They were wrestling with the ideas and working to build their own understanding of the SWH approach and then working to translate the meaning into their classroom as learning and teaching.

Watching the developmental process of the pilot teachers through their running dialogues in the margins was insightful and produced new perspective on how teachers may use the book to enhance learning in their students. As you read, *talk with the text*. Argue through the ideas and capture all of this in the margins. Talking to the text and capturing your thinking as you mentally process your own practice creates the sense of conversation that we have enjoyed while helping you build a stronger understanding of the issues and concepts that are discussed throughout the book. If you record your thoughts as you are presented with the theory in Part 1 of the book, you can return to these as you move through the book and gain a sense of your learning while appreciating the issues in a deeper and broader context. Invite your students and colleagues into the conversation. As you generate your own questions in working through the book ask those around you the same questions. Explain your ideas as they develop and talk about them. Translating your thinking into conversations will help you deepen your understanding and evaluate it at the same time. How many times in teaching a topic that you thought you understood have you found that you didn't understand nearly as well as you thought? The same principle will apply here, and by talking with others you will find what you understand in a much richer manner than keeping all the conversation inside your head.

Change is difficult. Change within today's high-pressure world of education is even more difficult. You are being challenged from all directions with the No Child Left Behind (NCLB) act, parents, administration, students, and community. Accountability is being demanded and tests proliferate. Mak-

**HAVE A GO! THE START OF YOUR JOURNEY**

When was the last time you were really challenged by professional development? If you are reading this book you probably are interested in your students' learning. Before beginning the book take some time and do an assessment of your classroom learning environment, your students' learning, and your teaching. This can serve as your baseline. In Appendix A, you will find a series of questions to guide you in thinking about your classroom learning environment, your students' learning, and your teaching.

ing a decision to begin any change effort in this atmosphere can be very frightening. But if you seriously ask yourself, "Is my teaching the best it can be, and are my students learning at the level they are capable of?" and your answer is "no," you as a conscientious professional have no choice but to take the risk and examine your own teaching process. To help make this change process more manageable we continually remind you through the book to be realistic and move in measured and practical steps. Don't try to change everything at once. All of us know that the road to success in adopting the SWH approach is a challenging course that takes time and work. Be patient, be realistic, and be honest.

In addition, to make this process an active learning experience for you as a teacher, we have provided "Have a Go" exercises designed to start you into an interactive process with the key points of each chapter. The exercises are short and ask you to engage in some thinking opportunities or conduct some learning experiments in your classes.

## About the Book

The book is divided into three sections. The first section provides some background into using the SWH approach. The authors believe it is essential that using the SWH approach requires much more than simply gaining a new strategy. We need to review our understanding of what learning is—is it transferring information? Is it about constructing knowledge? We need to examine how our view of learning matches up with our view of teaching. This section describes our perspectives on learning and teaching and how they are critical for using the SWH approach. The first section finishes with a discussion of language and its essential function in learning science.

The second section, which is structured on the student template, deals with the implementation of the SWH approach. Chapter 5 is an introduction. Chapter 6 introduces the concept of questions, claims, and evidence. Chapter 7 deals with reading and reflection, and Chapter 8 looks at pulling all the pieces together while preparing for the summary-writing experience. The intention of this section is to introduce the teaching approaches required when using the SWH approach.

The third section is framed around how to examine teaching practices when using the SWH as well as a review of frequently asked questions. Chapter 9 introduces a performance matrix that we have used throughout our studies when working with teachers. The intent of the matrix is to provide guidance to teachers as well as act as a tool to examine how well they believe they are implementing the SWH approach. Chapter 10 deals with frequently asked questions posed by teachers and an overview of the research that has been conducted on the SWH approach.

Particular features of this book include many opportunities to read the stories of teachers and students in science classrooms as well as pose some challenges to engage the reader through the pages of this book. Each of these special features is set off in the text. These features include:

TEACHER'S VOICE: We believe the teacher's voice is essential to our work, and we have included their stories of joys and struggles, aha moments, and frustration points to help describe in detail the implementation of the SWH approach.

FROM THE STUDENTS: Throughout the pages of this book, we will provide examples of student writing and student voices from inside classrooms to help you get an insider perspective on student learning.

SWH TOOLS: Over the past ten years, teachers and consultants who have worked with this approach have developed a variety of tools. Many of these tools are provided throughout the book to help you get started in implementing your own unit.

HAVE A GO: Finally, the book concludes with the "have a go" appendices. These featured activities are for the reader to try in and out of the classroom setting to engage in active learning experience around the implementation and examination of the SWH approach.

We have written the book with guidance from a group of teachers who have been using the SWH approach. They have provided insight and critical comments, making sure that we as authors are focusing on the realities of the classroom. We thank this group. Throughout the book we have included vignettes from teachers who have used the SWH approach, as well as provided examples of student work. We have done this to share voices from the classroom so that as a reader you can get a glimpse into what can and does happen when we get out of the way and let our students learn. We hope you enjoy the book and take the time to work through some of the suggestions and advice. Take this opportunity to use this approach that has been very beneficial for the teachers and students who have been using the Science Writing Heuristic around the world.

## Revisiting the Big Idea

The challenge has been set: Any new investigation or inquiry begins with a question. We began this introduction by stating that this book is not about teaching but rather about *learning*. Thus, the key question appears to be, "How do I teach science in the service of learning . . . where the learning for each of my students is maximized, providing opportunities not only to grow in their science understanding but to include opportunities to grow as readers, writers, and mathematicians?" Now, with our question in mind, let's begin this investigation.

# Examining Teaching in the Service of Learning

**From the Students**

I have to tell you the truth—at first I didn't like it a whole lot when my teacher said she was going to teach with this new thing called the Science Writing Heuristic. I am an "A" student and I know how to DO science. I read. I memorize. And I tell you what I know on a test. Simple. Now, with this heuristic, I have to think. I have to know and the answer isn't always simple. I hated it, but I have to admit, I think about it more and I realize that even when I memorized the answers, I didn't really understand what that meant or how I could use that information to understand. Like force and motion—like why my car holds tight on a curve or why the weight of a baseball matters in the way that I throw it. Science is not just a class I take now but I think about what it means outside the school all the time. I question everything and found out that there are no simple answers. I think that is a good thing. (Written anonymously by a high school student)

*continues on next page*

**Figure I.1.** *Students engaged in an SWH classroom*

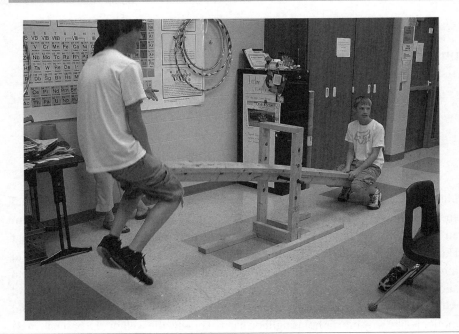

The above student's reflection on learning with the SWH approach is intriguing and opens up a discussion about what learning is and how we teach in a manner to support that learning. Ask yourself these questions:

How can I invigorate my classroom to create a dynamic learning space for all students?

How can I get more students involved in science inquiry and learning?

How can I help my students to improve their test scores?

What would make teaching more stimulating and engaging for me?

Answers to these questions will be revealed throughout the following pages. In this first section, the investigation begins with an overview of the SWH approach (Chapter 1), an examination of what needs to be known about learning (Chapter 2) and teaching (Chapter 3) to put the SWH approach to use in classrooms, and finally, to look at the role of writing in the science classroom (Chapter 4).

# Introduction to the Science Writing Heuristic (SWH) Approach

## Teacher's Voice

After a twenty-five-year career as a high school science teacher I was pretty much set in my ways of disseminating information to my students. We would have lecture/note taking, discussion, lab investigations, worksheets, cooperative learning groups, projects, and so on. It was not a bad classroom in my opinion: It was very organized. The activities were varied. I was trying to include all students by doing different activities and using a variety of methods that would incorporate the diverse learning styles of students.

But as the science teachers in our school began to learn about the SWH process and think about what learning and teaching were, we made some discoveries of our own. The key ones were that the students are in control of what they learn and that teaching can move from a method of giving information to a method of guiding students to build their knowledge based upon what they already know.

So we moved from how much material we could present to figuring out what was really important. We tried to come up with the "big ideas" for the units we were teaching. We found out what the students knew and modified the kinds of activities we were already doing so the students could explore, inquire, build on concepts of which they had some prior knowledge, and make connections.

To do this we were willing to change from a teacher-centered classroom to a student-centered classroom. We were asking the students to be more active and take control of their learning by posing questions, exploring, discussing, and writing about what they discovered. As teachers we were also becoming more active as we designed units that would engage the students and exploring ways to make the units meaningful. What do we want students to know and how are we going to accomplish that? What kinds of questions can we ask? How do we get all students involved? We planned for these things, but each day as I got up to get ready for school the process of getting students involved was on my mind. The process was making me think about teaching. I get up in the morning and am always thinking about exactly how things are going to go. You know, you are really thinking more about your subject matter than before. That is different. You are trying to come up with better ways of posing questions to students.

What is so good about this approach? Seeing students design experiments to answer a question that they want to know about. Seeing students who do not usually say much actually have an opinion that others listen to and think about. Seeing students research what others have done to answer a question similar to theirs. Seeing students express what they have found out with the written word. Seeing students discuss, argue, or debate points of view. Seeing students make connections with their world and the world of science. Students are in control of their learning—we finally began to understand that we never really had control even though we thought we did. We can guide them so that they have a real stake in the learning process.

**HAVE A GO! YOUR TEACHER VOICE**

If you were to write your own first paragraph as you enter this process, how would it compare to the teacher above? If you are new in your career, in the mid-years, or a seasoned veteran, what would you say about yourself? Appendix B will help you form your own beginning paragraph for your SWH journey.

The teacher's voice from the passage at the beginning of the chapter may sound like you. This is from an actual teacher who is in the process of implementing the SWH and becoming a better teacher of science. Like so many teachers, this teacher had what would be described by almost all observers as a good classroom. The teacher was doing all the "right" things, the class climate would be seen by most as excellent, and teacher evaluations were outstanding. But here is a teacher nearing the end of his career who had a sense that something was missing. Are you confident that your classroom provides for the best learning possible for your students? If you are like this teacher and sense that something is lacking, take the time and effort to work through this book with your classroom and you may find yourself making the same comments in a few years about your students.

## What Is the SWH Approach?

So, what is the process that is supposed to help students learn science better? How do we encourage our students to pose questions and explore their answers while better representing that learning on standardized tests? Why is there a need to move away from the traditional approaches to science teaching? We know that the number of students moving into science and science-based careers is decreasing—why? Many factors are present, but as science educators we have to ask ourselves, "What are we doing in our classrooms that does not promote, encourage, and stimulate students to consider and choose careers in science?"

When considering why this lack of interest in science exists, we need to look critically at the approaches to science teaching and learning that have historically permeated our work. Traditional science laboratory activities are structured around the laboratory report format. Students are expected to engage in a format that outlines the hypothesis, procedures, observations, results, and discussion. Unfortunately, scientists use this format not in the laboratory but primarily to report their work in journals for publication. In the lab, they pose questions, make claims, gather evidence, debate with each other, compare their answers with others in the field, and attempt to look for patterns across their results. Scientists are engaged in argumentation—at the very core of science activity is scientific argument. Having completed this process of argument, scientists then prepare their written reports for publication.

While a great deal of work has been done on examining the strategies required by teachers to be successful when using inquiry, there are still two areas of concern. The first is that there has been a lack of emphasis on argumentation; the second is that there has been very limited or almost no focus on language and science. To address these concerns, Carolyn Keys and Brian Hand in 1997 developed the Science Writing Heuristic (SWH) as an approach to use in school classrooms (see Figure 1.1).

The SWH approach consists of a framework to guide activities as well as a "metacognitive" support, or support of thinking and discussion about thinking, to prompt student reasoning about data. Similar to Gowin's Vee heuristic (1981, p. 157), the SWH approach provides learners with a heuristic template or plan to guide science activity and reasoning in writing. Further, the SWH approach provides teachers with a template of suggested strategies to enhance learning from laboratory activities. As a whole, the activities and metacognitive scaffolds seek to provide authentic meaning-making opportunities for learners. The negotiation of meaning occurs across multiple formats for discussion and writing. The SWH process is conceptualized as a bridge between informal, expressive writing modes that foster personally constructed science understandings and more formal, public modes that focus on canonical forms of reasoning in science. In this way, the heuristic scaffolds learners in both understanding their own lab activity and connecting this knowledge to other science ideas. The template or plan for student thinking (see Figure 1.1) prompts learners to generate questions, claims, and evidence for those claims. It also asks them to compare their laboratory findings with others, including their peers and information in the textbook, Internet, or other sources. The template for student thinking also

**Figure 1.1.** *The Science Writing Heuristic teacher and student templates*

| The Science Writing Heuristic, Part I | The Science Writing Heuristic, Part II |
|---|---|
| **A plan for teacher-designed activities to promote laboratory understanding** | **A plan for students** |
| 1. Exploration of preinstruction understanding through individual or group concept mapping | 1. Beginning ideas—What are my questions? |
| 2. Pre-laboratory activities, including informal writing, making observations, brainstorming, and posing questions | 2. Tests—What did I do? |
| 3. Participation in laboratory activity | 3. Observations—What did I see? |
| 4. Negotiation phase I—Writing personal meanings for laboratory activity (for example, writing journals) | 4. Claims—What can I claim? |
| 5. Negotiation phase II—Sharing and comparing data interpretations in small groups (for example, making group charts) | 5. Evidence—How do I know? Why am I making these claims? |
| 6. Negotiation phase III—Comparing science ideas to textbooks or other printed resources (for example, writing group notes in response to focus questions) | 6. Reading—How do my ideas compare with others' ideas? |
| 7. Negotiation phase IV—Individual reflection and writing (for example, creating a presentation such as a poster or report for a larger audience) | 7. Reflection—How have my ideas changed? |
| 8. Exploration of postinstruction understanding through concept mapping | |

prompts learners to reflect on how their own ideas have changed during the experience of the laboratory activity. The SWH approach to teaching science includes what can be understood as an alternative format for laboratory reports. Instead of responding to the five traditional sections—purpose, methods, observations, results, and conclusions—students are expected to respond to prompts eliciting questioning, knowledge claims, evidence, description of data and observations, and methods and to reflect on changes to their own thinking. At first glance these may appear to be the same but in reality they are quite different. The differences will become evident as you read this book.

While the SWH recognizes the need for students to conduct laboratory investigations that develop an understanding of scientific methods and procedures, the teacher's template or plan also seeks to provide a stronger pedagogical focus for this learning. In other words, the SWH approach is based on the assumption that science writing tasks in school should reflect some of the characteristics of scientists' writing but also be shaped as teaching tools to encourage students to "unpack" scientific meaning and reasoning. The SWH approach is intended to promote both scientific thinking and reasoning in the laboratory, as well as metacognition, where learners become aware of the basis of their knowledge and are able to monitor their learning more explicitly. Because the SWH approach focuses on canonical forms of scientific thinking, such as the development of links between claims and evidence, it also has the potential to build learners' understanding of the nature of science, strengthen conceptual understandings, and engage them in authentic argumentation process of science.

The SWH approach emphasizes the collaborative nature of scientific activity, that is, scientific argumentation, where learners are expected to engage in a continuous cycle of negotiating and clarifying meanings and explanations with their peers and teacher. In other words, the SWH approach is designed to promote classroom discussion where students' personal explanations and observations are tested against the perceptions and contributions of the broader group. Learners are encouraged to make explicit and defensible connections between questions, observations, data, claims, and evidence. When students state a claim for an investigation, they are expected to describe a pattern, make a generalization, state a relationship, or construct an explanation.

The SWH approach promotes students' participation in setting their own investigative agenda for laboratory work, framing questions, proposing methods to address these questions, and carrying out appropriate investigations. Such an approach to laboratory work is advocated in many national science curriculum documents on the grounds that this freedom of choice will promote greater student engagement and motivation with topics (NRC, 1996). However, in practice, laboratory work often follows a narrow teacher agenda that does not allow for broader questioning or more diverse data interpretation. When procedures are uniform for all students, where data are similar, and where claims match expected outcomes, then the reportage of results and conclusions often seems meaningless to students and lacks opportunities for deeper student learning about the topic or for developing scientific reasoning skills. (If everyone gets the same answer why ask the question? How meaningful is this type of experience? Is this just another school exercise done *to* them?) To address these issues, the SWH approach is designed to provide scaffolding for purposeful thinking about the relationships between questions, evidence, and claims.

## Revisiting the Big Idea

The SWH approach was designed to create experiences for students to engage in science inquiry and to use language similar to the variety of ways scientists use multiple forms of language to describe, discuss, and understand their thinking. Not only does this approach build curriculum and understanding around students' prior knowledge and their own questions about the topic, the SWH is designed to promote classroom discussion where students' personal explanations and observations

---

### From the Students

In this sixth-grade classroom, after completing a tug-of-war competition with their group-created robots, several student scientists were frustrated by their inability to justify why one robot beat another. As they started to throw around their theories, they formulated the question: What variables actually affected robot power?

This question led them to design and conduct their own investigation to determine what variables made one robot more powerful than another. These student-scientists asked their own testable question, created their own investigation plan, and conducted several tests to find the answer to their question. Even as they encountered several snags and setbacks (like finding out they changed more than one variable or that gears could actually shoot off a robot), they were determined to find the answers to their many questions and worked very hard to uncover the answers behind the mystery of power.

Once these student-scientists had the data they were looking for, they began to evaluate what it could do to answer their questions. After days of graphing and discussion, the student-scientists formulated claims supported by evidence from their investigation and wrote these articles to enlighten their audience (parents, family, and friends) about the mystery of power. One example entry from the magazine can be found in Figure 1.2.

*continues on next page*

**Figure 1.2.** *Students in a sixth-grade classroom create a class magazine to share the results of an SWH investigation related to their questions about robotics*

2 0 0 8 · A P R I L · E D I T I O N

the

# WEIGHT UPDATE

EVER WONDER HOW WEIGHT AFFECTS POWER?

*Weights Used*

Hi, we're group #14 and our question was how does weight affect the power of your robot? We set out to see how weight affects the power of our robot, so come along with us on our journey to answer the big question of group #14.

## TEST STEPS

The first thing we did was build the tracker from our Lego Mindstorms manual. Then we placed two pieces of tape 1 meter apart and we attached a clipboard to the robot. We made sure that the robot could pull the clipboard. Then we put a 12 ounce can of Cherry Coke on the clipboard and kept adding cans until the robot could not pull any more. That was the test. Then we recorded our data. We did the same thing again but added 200 grams to the robot and tested. Then we recorded our data and did the same thing again, this time adding 400 and 600 grams of weight.

For our robot design, we built the tracker from our Lego Mindstorms manual and added a 6-centimeter wide box to the tracker. The box was 9 Legos high and the Legos were each a centimeter high. The string was attached to two sticks on either side of the front of the robot.

*continues on next page*

**Figure 1.2.** *(Continued)*

## Test details and results

In the test, the 482.8g robot (no added weight) had a hard time pulling 1 can but did successfully pull it. The 682.5g robot (200g added) pulled 1 can, 2 cans and 1 again. The 682.5g robot had trouble pulling 2 cans but did it. The 882.8g (400g added) pulled 1 can and then 2 cans, but with 3 it wouldn't even budge. It just pulled 2 cans with more power. The 1,082.8g robot (600g added) pulled 2 cans but didn't pull any more because it had trouble pulling itself.

### Test results

In the test, the robots with the total weight of 882.8g and 1,082.8g pulled and average of 2 cans of pop, and the robots with the weight of 482.8g total and 682.5g pulled an average of 1 can of pop. In the test, 482.8g pulled 1 can on all the tests, 682.5g pulled 1 can on the first test, 2 cans on the second test and 1 can on the 3rd test, 882.8g pulled 2 cans on the first test, 1 can on the second test and 2 cans on the last test, and 1,082.8g pulled 2 cans on all the tests.

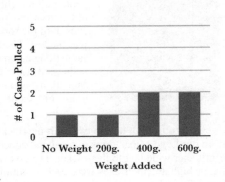

*continues on next page*

**Figure 1.2.** *(Continued)*

## Claim & Evidence

**Claim**: Our claim is that weight DOES affect the success of your robot, and that 400g. and 600g. of extra weight are the best amounts of extra weight.

**Evidence**: We know our claim is right because we did some tests to see what amount of extra weight has the most power. We did this by seeing how many pop cans the robot could pull. After that we made a bar graph to display the data of our tests. The graph said that no extra weight and 200g. of extra weight could both pull an average of 1 can. The graph also said that 400g. and 600g. of extra weight both pulled an average of 2 cans. This clearly proves that the amount of extra weight DOES make a difference in the success of your robot, and that 400g. and 600g. of extra weight are the best amounts of extra weight to have.

## Reflection

In our test, we thought that 400g. added weight would be the best, because it's not too much weight and not to little. We soon found out that we were right and 400g. added weight was one of the best. 600g. added weight was good too, but weighed to much to pull itself sometime. No added weight and 200g. added weight was not enough weight to cause good traction, so they had a average of 1 can.

## Closing

After all of this testing, recording, and graphing, we're still wondering: Would our results have been different if we had used different wheels or a different power level? You can create your own tests and graphs like we did. There are tons of variables that you can test yourself. You can even do the tests we did and see if you get the same results. It doesn't take much, all you need to do is put your mind to it, get some friends to help you, and you can easily get the results.

*continues on next page*

**Figure 1.2.** *(Continued)*

# Tracks Vs. Wheels

## Our question was: <u>What had the best traction? Wheels or Tracks?</u>

April 18, 2008

Anything wheels can do tracks can do better!

(Side view of robot with tracks)

Never try small wheels in front and medium wheels in back, because it won't go anywhere!

(Front view of robot with big wheels)

CAUTION!!!!!!!

Tracks are very powerful!!!!!!!

(Top view of robot with grip wheels)

## Plan

1. Build robot tracker with tracks from Lego Mindstorms manual
2. Make program
3. Test robot, start out with 1 can, if it pulls add more cans
4. Collect data to see how many cans are pulled

5. Build tracker robot with BIG wheels from Lego Mindstorms manual
6. Test robot, start out with one can then add more cans if it pulls across the floor, add more cans until it can't pull anymore
7. Collect data from test; see how many cans it pulled
8. Build robot with medium wheels in front and small wheels in back
9. Test robot, start out with clipboard then start adding cans
10. Collect data; see how many cans it pulled
11. Small wheels in front medium wheels in back
12. Test with clipboard, and then start out with MORE cans

13. Collect data; see how many cans it pulled
14. Build robot with medium grip wheels
15. Start to test with clipboard, and then add one can, until it can't pull anymore
16. Collect data see how many cans it pulled
17. Build robot with BIG wheels
18. Test robot with clipboard then starts adding cans
19. Collect data to see how many cans it pulled
20. Average each test

*continues on next page*

**Figure 1.2.** *(Continued)*

# Graph

- Tracks
- Medium Wheels in Front Small Wheels in back
- Grip Wheels
- Big Wheels
- Small Wheels in front Medium wheels in back

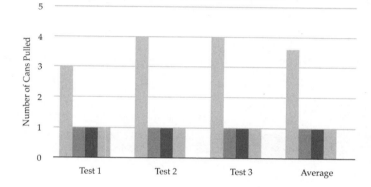

## Claim, Evidence, And Reflection

### Claim

The item with the best traction is tracks.

### Evidence

Tracks had the best traction with an average of 3.6 cans pulled. Medium wheels in front, small wheels in back had an average of 1 can pulled.

Small wheels in front, medium wheels in back had an average 0 cans pulled. Grip wheels had an average of 1 can pulled and big wheels also had an average of 1 can pulled. The tracks, when we were testing, had a lot of connection with the ground, creating more friction. All of the other ones tested kept slipping on the ground and didn't get very good connection with the carpet. Since there was no connection between the wheels and the ground, they could not pull any cans and could not get a high average.

### Reflection

I think that our tests went great. We had to fix a lot of gears coming off, but we took care of that right away. Sometimes the string came off, so we took the string and placed it in a between two Lego's. It worked much better!

**Remember with great traction comes great power!**

are tested against the perceptions and contributions of the broader group. Learners are encouraged to make explicit and defensible connections between questions, observations, data, claims, and evidence. Students use diverse forms of language (written, oral, pictorial, and numeric) to describe a pattern, make a generalization, state a relationship, or construct an explanation. The template (in Figure 1.1) provides a plan for student investigation and a complementary teacher plan for helping students negotiate meaning throughout the SWH investigation.

# CHAPTER 2

# What Do We Have to Know?
## (Theory and Practice)

One of the most common areas of discussions when talking with teachers is about their role in the classroom. As educators we focus a great deal of attention on what we have to do on a daily basis. From the preservice teacher to the experienced teacher, we all see our role as helping students to learn and to become valuable, contributing members of society. We all work hard at developing our teaching skills so that we can assist students to develop as learners over the year. An important question that we need to deal with is how much time should we spend on exploring the second component of what occurs in a classroom teaching and learning, that is, learning? What do we really understand about learning, and how is this related to teaching?

## A Starting Point

In beginning discussions on learning, it is crucial to begin with examining what we know about ourselves as learners. When was the last time that we sat down and thought through the conditions that we require for ourselves as learners—not as teachers but as adults learning something new? Try completing the following task: Write down the five most important criteria that you require when you are learning something (for example, a hobby). See if your answers match these common responses:

❖ Time to explore on my own

❖ Opportunities to ask experts

❖ The right equipment available to use

❖ Interest in the topic

❖ Opportunities to practice

❖ Ability to control the pace of learning

These responses seem to be straightforward and reasonable. It is *very rare* that responses are:

❖ Be told exactly what to do

❖ Answer questions out of the textbook

❖ Write chapter summaries

❖ Take the expert's notes down word for word

The immediate question is: Why do we fail to put the strategies into our own classrooms that we want for ourselves when we learn? Of course, the response is often "Yeah, but we have to . . ." Think about two challenges to this thinking. First, why is it that whenever someone talks to a group of people or shows a group of people a new skill, no two people in the group repeat the message or skill in exactly the same manner as the person who was in charge? Second, why is it that all students are not succeeding equally well if the current strategies implemented mean that as teachers we control the information they receive? With these questions in mind, let's explore the act of teaching and learning in relation to current theory and practice.

**HAVE A GO!**
**ALIGNING LEARNING AND TEACHING**

As you look at the questions about learning and your answers, do they align? Do you take into account your own learning when you teach your students? Go to Appendix C to explore these ideas.

## Learning

Two quotes are important when we talk about learning. The first is by Strike (1987, p. 483) who stated, "philosophically the suggestion that people are active in learning or knowledge construction is rather uninteresting. It is uninteresting because almost no one, beyond a few aberrant behaviorists, denies it." This quote sets the stage for our thinking over the last fifteen years and underpins the basis for all the curriculum reform documents brought out in the '90s. The National Science Education Standards (NRC, 1996) places great emphasis on the need for students to be active learners, to inquire and be curious about science, and to communicate their understandings to others. Constructivist learning theory has been the big buzzword in science education and is often used within these curriculum documents. This theory is one example of cognitive learning theory.

The question becomes, what is cognitive theory? If one builds from Strike's quote then we accept that cognitive theory focuses on the broad concept that each individual is active in a process of constructing knowledge. Many different theories have been put forward under the broad umbrella of cognitive theory, such as information processing, radical constructivism, social constructivism, interactive constructivism, and developmental theory, to name a few. It is not our intention to discuss these in detail but rather to discuss some of the terms that are often brought forward in discussions on learning. If we are asked to draw a concept map of what we understand by learning, what would be some of the terms that we would need to, or think we should, put down? Without going back to the psychology 101 books—and, yes, we do remember names such as Piaget, Vygotsky, and others—the bigger question here is: What did they say? Have a go here and see what you can remember. How many terms can you remember? If we generated a list of terms, maybe a few words such as these would appear:

❖ Learning

❖ Understanding

❖ Conceptual frameworks

❖ Assimilation

❖ Accommodation

❖ Disequilibrium

❖ Conceptual change

How are these words connected and what do they really mean? Let's start with *learning* and *understanding*—these are not the same. Within the education psychology community, *learning* is defined as when somebody has gained some knowledge, either a skill or some content material. *Understanding* refers to the ability of the learner to transfer the knowledge to new and different situations. The authors of the National Science Education Standards recognized this difference when they suggested that the central goal of science teaching is having "students learn scientific knowledge with understanding" (NRC, 1996, p. 21). These differences in terminology are important because they begin to shape what we understand and practice in the classroom.

In this discussion, we are focusing on understanding, that is, the building of conceptual frameworks or schemas, which learners can use in any situation they wish. Our current understanding of knowledge storage is that we have conceptual frames or schema to store knowledge. A conceptual framework is viewed as an interconnected "web" of knowledge built around a single concept. For example, if we say the word *fishing*, then automatically we have a series of images, words, and ideas that are connected and define our individual understandings of fishing. These understandings differ between people, for example, people who live in desert climates with no familiarity of frozen lakes and streams would be unlikely to incorporate concepts of ice fishing in their conceptual frameworks. Every individual has his or her unique conceptual framework, that is, everyone stores knowledge in a unique web based on background knowledge and environments. Even though we may all receive the exact same message or content knowledge, we will interact with this knowledge in slightly different ways because our conceptual frameworks are not identical.

What does it mean to interact with this knowledge? Cognitive theories of learning are based on the notion that a learner has to negotiate meaning, that is, a learner has his or her own knowledge that will interact with the new knowledge to increase the total amount of knowledge stored. The learner has to negotiate with himself or herself on the individual level and across the various groups of people that he or she will interact with daily. For example, when studying force the student has to negotiate what he or she understands about the word, negotiate what meaning the teacher in the science classroom brings to the word, and negotiate with family members and with peers when in after-school activities. In each of these contexts, the meaning of the word *force* can vary and the individual has to be able to negotiate a meaning of the word depending on the context. Parents can force students to "clean their bedroom," but this does not mean the teacher's concept of Newton's First Law is being applied to this act of cleaning.

When we ask learners to read a textbook about force, we are asking them to negotiate meaning from the text. They have to negotiate between their own knowledge and what the text is telling them. Similarly, when writing learners must negotiate meaning between what is personally known and what one believes the audience can understand. It is important for us to recognize that this process of negotiation is constant; knowledge is not simply passed from one person to another. While we may believe that we have provided a clear and simple explanation of a concept, each learner must go through an individual process of negotiation to arrive at an understanding. Students can take notes and give us back what we want to hear but that does not mean this knowledge is stored in long-term memory. This concept of social negotiation of meaning was one of the important contributions of Lev Vygotsky (1978) to understanding the dynamic nature of learning.

If learning is about the negotiation of meaning, is there a particular process required to move from students learning the concept to constructing an understanding of the concept? Since the mid-1980s, science education has been guided in great part by the idea of a conceptual change process. To successfully negotiate meaning requires that the learner construct a richer version of the concept, that is, the individual's conceptual framework is different than when he or she first started the inquiry process.

## Teacher's Voice

Previously the students wanted to hear what you had to say and they wrote down what you said and read the assigned pages. They would always get their As in that way and they seem to learn very well. Now this makes them work a little bit more. They have to really think more, because they are having input into directing the sequence of the lesson. I think it is better for the learning process. They get the point pretty well and they accept this. This is the way it's going to be. They adapted.

This is different for me. I think this is the big change for me—I was directing the learning, they were the learners. Now we are trying to have them, I think, go where they want to go on the learning and that is still difficult. They have more ownership of the classes. That was hard for me because before it was me most of the time, I thought I controlled the knowledge, I had the ownership.

### HAVE A GO!
### NEGOTIATING YOUR OWN MEANING

So often you hear people say that the best way to learn something is to teach it. This is an example of negotiating meaning. Have a go with Appendix D to look more closely at the negotiation of meaning.

## Teacher's Voice

"Oh, you know what I am trying to say?" I heard this over and over in my classroom prior to engaging in the SWH approach. The students weren't able to clearly articulate their ideas, and I usually responded by saying yes and then completing what I thought their thought should be. I was denying the student the opportunity to complete their negotiation phase. They obviously hadn't negotiated an adequate meaning and I interrupted the process.

# Conceptual Change

To begin, we all have some basic understanding of a topic, however disconnected it is, or conversely, the only framework that we have to look at a topic that is completely foreign to us is the one that exists in our head. That is, we will examine a topic using the frameworks that already exist in our heads. For example, if we do not have a chemistry background and someone talks about equilibrium, we do not have any idea what this concept is or what possible questions we could ask about the topic. However, we know what the term *equal* means or what an equals sign represents based on our prior knowledge and experiences. Thus, we tend to look at the topic of equilibrium based on our concept of equal, which initially would appear to have no connections to chemical reactions and equations. To build a rich understanding as opposed to rote or memorized learning concepts of equilibrium means that new knowledge being introduced has to be connected in some manner to our existing conceptual frameworks. The question becomes, how do we build on our existing conceptual framework?

Any decision to change a framework is the decision of the individual. It is the individual who makes a choice to add to, delete from, or keep unchanged his or her framework. We as teachers do not have any control of what goes on inside anyone's head. *As teachers we can control the environment but not the cognitive activities of an individual.* Thus, for individuals to change what they believe they need to make some decisions about how satisfied they are with what they know when they begin to examine a new topic or idea. Such words as *disequilibrium, dissatisfaction*, and *perturbation* have been used to describe the condition that learners undergo when faced with something that is new or different to what they currently believe. To change existing schema, learners need to feel as though what they currently believe will not adequately address the problem or the topic they are currently engaged with at the time. Teaching then involves setting up the classroom experiences in a way that creates the situation where the student is no longer satisfied with their existing schema. Simply having an external source stating that they are wrong is no condition for achieving change. Evidence of this is the lack of success we have with students who cannot seem to understand an idea no matter how many times as teacher you tell them.

Therefore, the first step in getting learners to undergo some conceptual change is for individuals to begin to be dissatisfied with what they currently believe. Does this mean that they will automatically adopt the new knowledge that is "fed into the system?" If it were that easy, our jobs would be so much simpler! Who, then, makes the decision about how valid the new knowledge is that individuals deal with while engaged in the learning process? We will keep reiterating that it is the individual who makes decisions about the value of the new knowledge. Conceptual change theorists use the terms *plausible* and *intelligible* to describe the conditions required by the learner. These conditions refer to the concept that the new knowledge not only makes sense but also appears to be true or have value. Why do learners have difficulty grasping science concepts when we as teachers have made a logical presentation? Has it made sense to the learners? Why do advertisers have so much success? Mainly because they appeal to the perceived needs or wants of the buyer who then believes that what is being presented is true. How many weight-loss diets or how many different types of exercise equipment have been sold because buyers believe that what is being said applies to them and the claims, therefore, are true?

Having made a decision that the new ideas are valuable and make sense, will the learner use them? There is no definite black-and-white answer to this. The conceptual change theory uses terms like *fruitful* and *feasible* to explain this phase of learner use. By this they mean that learners will use the new ideas if these ideas begin to solve problems for them in ways that their old ideas did not. Does this mean that the new concepts become part of the learner's conceptual framework? Current thinking suggests that this takes time and repeated use across a number of different situations. In essence, a competition is going on between old and new concepts. If the new concept can solve more problems or be applied to more situations more often, then it will become the dominant one within the learner's framework.

How does this new knowledge fit into existing frameworks? Much discussion has taken place about what occurs. Two terms put forward by Piaget (Piaget and Inhelder, 1969), *assimilation* and *accommodation*, attempt to provide an explanation for what occurs for the learner. In terms of the change to existing frameworks, the question revolves around the degree of change that is needed. This becomes important in using the Piagetian terms. If the learner is adding new knowledge to the framework that is not radical but rather extends or strengthens the framework, then we tend to say that this knowledge is assimilated into the existing framework. By this we mean that the learner is not making a significant change to what he or she believes. However, if what is required is a completely new "branch" of the framework to be developed, then we tend to use the term *accommodation*. The learner is required to accommodate a different branch of the framework that will be in competition with the existing branch dealing with the particular phenomena or problem. It is important to understand that accommodation is not a spontaneous thing. It does take time and repeated use of the new branch of the framework. Again, we reiterate—*the learner is the one making the decisions about his or her own framework and how much repeated use is required to have final acceptance of the idea.*

In summary, understanding is about individuals engaging their conceptual frameworks in an attempt to use new knowledge across a broad range of situations. Learners are trying to negotiate meaning or make meaning from the situations that they face, and the only real "filter" they have is their own conceptual framework.

## Teaching

A second quote builds on this body of knowledge, although it was first used in the '60s. David Ausubel, a psychologist, discussed through his work that the single most important thing in education is to find out what the child knows and teach him or

**Figure 2.1.** *An SWH investigation by a sixth-grade student that shows the development of conceptual understanding related to her question about erosion*

## Science Writing Heuristic

**1) What is my question?**
**What natural cause ( slope amount of water moisture content affect the amount of erosion in a landscape?**

**2) What did I do?**
**First we put plastic over our desk's. Then we got a stream table with a mixture of sand and clay, and set it on the plastic on a ruler ( 20" across). After that we put a cup half on the stream edge and half on ruler, then we moved the duck tape off. Then we poured the water into the cup.**

**3)What did I see?**

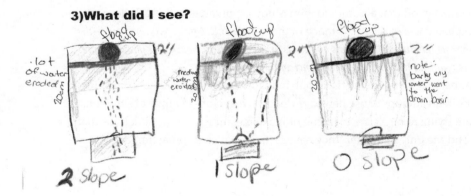

*continues on next page*

Figure 2.1. *(Continued)*

**4) What is my claim?**
**I found that using two barriers of slop and**
**moist earth materials provided most erosion in**
**our steam table.**

**5) What is my evidence?**
**I drew drawings of my evidence and compared**
**them to other tables.**

**6) What do others say? The continents are**
**moving even though you don't see it moving.**
**The inside earth has four  layers. The center is**
**the enter core, is solid iron and nickel.**

**7) Have my ideas changed.**
**I have learned that on our steam table, the**
**flood cup makes it flood more than the**
**standard cup. yes my ideas have changed.**

*(apitlization (ed)*

her from there (1968). We personally believe that this thinking should guide all teaching. If we believe what was said earlier, then by necessity we have to engage with the second quote. If learning, leading to understanding, requires that individuals engage their conceptual frameworks and extend these, then teaching must be oriented to these frameworks. We need to remember that teaching does not occur in isolation to learning.

If we as teachers have no control over what is going on inside an individual's head, then we have to be able to engage with learners in ways that feature their knowledge at the center of the conversation. For how long have we heard that as teachers we tend to pitch our lesson at the middle group to be reasonably confident that we can get to most of the students? Didactic teaching tends to be the passing of information from the teacher to the students, that is, we teachers act as gatekeepers of knowledge. We parcel out what we think the students can handle. We judge that by making sure when we question students they can give us back what we have given out. While we are not suggesting that there is not a place for the giving out of information, we will discuss later how that should be done differently than what is generally the process with the goal to be contributing to student learning rather than being information memorized—and then forgotten. If learning is about having to negotiate meaning—that is, the process of examining and changing our frameworks—then teaching ought to provide learners with opportunities to do this. The first thing that we teachers need to do is to determine what students know about a topic. We need to play with a number of strategies that allow students to present in the public forum what they know about the topic. Much has been written about such strategies, so we will not expand greatly on these at this time. However, some strategies are Predict, Observe, Explain (POE) activities that require learners to predict what will happen, observe the activity, and then try to explain the result. In most cases they struggle with explanation or have elaborate nonscientifically acceptable explanations. Another activity that is used extensively in the elementary area but rarely at the high school level is the KWL activity. Students are asked what they *Know* about the topic, what they *Want* to learn about the topic, and on review, what they *Learned* about the topic.

The difficult thing for teachers from this point is how to plan for the rest of the unit. We tend to plan a unit based on how we think the unit should go or as outlined in the textbook. An important question for us is, how can we plan a unit when we do not know what the students know or where the students are in their understanding? Planning a unit without first finding out what the students know is a bit backward. Those teachers who have taught for many years tend to build intuitive understandings of what troubles students have with a topic but that does not mean that we know what this year's students are like or what their knowledge is in relation to the topic or unit.

## Teacher's Voice

So, I know when we start a unit we have put down the type of things we expect and how we are going to get there. However, until we determine what the students know we do not know the direction to go. I think our biggest thing is to say, "Okay, well, you guys know this" and allow them to lead you to a path that we need to go. Thus, every day as I am preparing for class to come in, I am always thinking about what would be a good question for leading them in the right direction. It is a lot of mental preparation for me (negotiating what they know and how I can question them to move them forward), but I just feel like we are spending more time on the main ideas now than we did in the past, where we would spend much more time on vocabulary and so forth.

## From the Students

**Figure 2.2.** *Poster created by students to reveal their process as they begin a new SWH investigation*

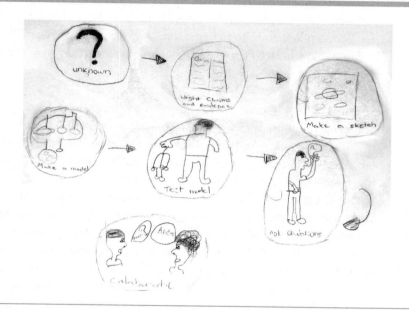

"Yeah, but that means that we will have twenty-five different kids with twenty-five different ideas. . . ." The rebuttal to this statement is—yes, there are twenty-five individuals but research indicates that students tend to cluster around some commonly held understandings and/or misunderstandings, some of which are more or less consistent with scientific explanations. While each student is an individual, from a conceptual viewpoint there tends to be only a few major groupings within a single class. Any one of these scientific misunderstandings can be used as a starting point of a unit. Remember, these conceptual viewpoints will be where some of the students are at, and others are not offering up excellent opportunities for negotiation through scientific argumentation. Students as a whole can then begin to appreciate that their knowledge is going to be challenged and built upon through class experiences. With the understanding of the issue of control, a shift occurs in a classroom that puts the learners in a position of power and they have the freedom to start to negotiate meaning from wherever their understanding is at that moment. If the classroom experiences are focused on these few major groupings, the learners can engage from their starting point.

## Teacher's Voice

For a lot of years I felt that kids could turn out the written experience, but I never got an understanding of their learning and where they were in their understanding and even their weaknesses and misconceptions. Through reading the heuristic assignments when they handed in the final products, they all had misconceptions and I had a better clue of where kids were mentally in their understanding. In fact, I felt so comfortable with where they were at that I did not administer a final exam.

Building on these ideas, planning needs to focus on the concepts or big ideas that frame the unit. *Learning is about understanding concepts, thus teaching must be about concepts* not *content.* To understand any concepts we need to build in the relevant content. We need to challenge students' conceptual understandings, not their rote learning of content. Examples of planning around the big ideas of science are discussed in the next chapter. By asking students to focus on the concepts framing the topic, we provide opportunities for students to match how they learn with how they store knowledge. Much of what is currently done in terms of information transfer strategies is that by the end of the unit the students are suppose to have an aha moment—the point at which the students have been able to build the content into some form of conceptual understanding. For the many students who never come to terms with science, a major factor is that they never get to understand how all these ideas and content fit together. We need to match how we learn with how we teach so that all students will have the opportunity to develop this understanding of science.

## Revisiting the Big Idea

We need to focus on two major cognitive ideas within science classrooms. First, every individual's learning is an activity that is undertaken by the individual over which we as teachers have no control. Learning is an activity that is controlled by an individual, not the teacher. Second, knowledge is stored in long-term memory as conceptual frameworks, not as separate content-knowledge points. The function of learning leading to understanding is to develop and enrich one's conceptual frameworks.

# From the Students

**Figure 2.3.** *Concept map created through a socially negotiated process by a group of sixth-grade students*

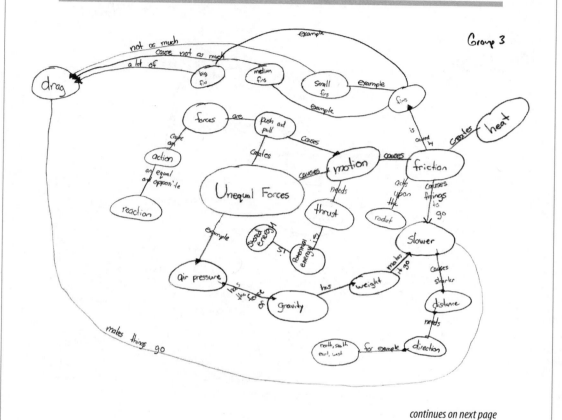

*continues on next page*

**Figure 2.3.** *(Continued)*

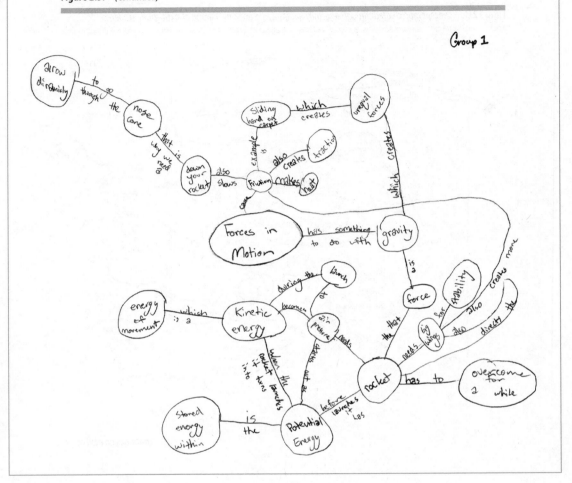

Group 1

# CHAPTER 3

# Teaching Skills Key to the SWH Approach

f teaching is to be aligned with learning as discussed in Chapter 2, what does that mean for us as teachers of science? If we follow the two major ideas that a learner is the only person who controls what goes on inside his or her head, and that knowledge is stored in conceptual frameworks, what does that imply about the pedagogical (teaching) skills that need to be developed? What do we need to change from what we are doing now? What are the key areas that we need to work on? We believe that there are five essential skills: 1) Determining the big idea(s) for the topic; 2) planning the learning activities; 3) finding out what students know; 4) questioning; and 5) group work. These skills and strategies are discussed in the following pages. However, we would first highlight the important concept that teaching is separate to management. Teacher-centered, teacher-controlled classrooms are designed first to manage the students and second to promote learning. Learning and teaching are not about managing students; you have to have good management strategies in place to implement cognitively based learning strategies. However, they are two different concepts—poor management leads to student and teacher frustration and poor learning. Ask yourself the question, have you had major management problems when the students have been engaged in answering their own questions and constructing knowledge for themselves?

## Determining the Big Idea(s) for the Topic

As teachers we have based our unit planning on the material that has to be addressed within any one topic. Given the textbook-based curricula in the various states, this is made a little easier because all the major content is highlighted in bold lettering within the text and teacher guides. The emphasis from the majority of textbook publishers is on making the curriculum material "teacher proof" so that it will be delivered "correctly" to students. Thus, the unit to be taught is basically framed around the content headings and chapter summaries. The idea of having the material linked in a conceptual manner is attempted by asking the learner to complete the concept map at the end of the chapter; by the way, in many cases, the map is laid out already with a "fill in the blanks" approach.

National and state standards are based on creating curricula that center learning around the big ideas of the science discipline area. How do we translate these into our classrooms? The single most important task is to determine the "big ideas" that are to be dealt with in the topic or unit, that is, what is (are) the major concept(s) that

## From the Students

In the example in Figure 3.1, a student has put together a concept map representing her understanding about unequal forces. Her map reveals her current conceptual framework and how she is developing her understanding of the big idea of the topic: forces and motion.

**Figure 3.1.** *Concept map on forces*

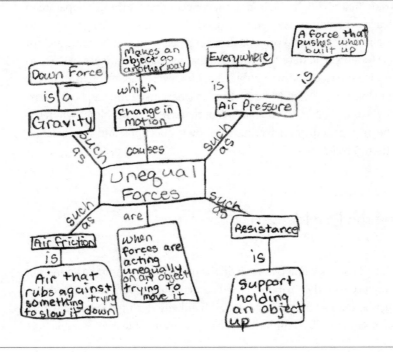

you want the students to understand by the end of the unit. Not the content items, not the list of facts, but the big idea that the students can use wherever they go. The guiding principle here is: *what is the major idea about the topic that you want your students to have when they leave your classroom after the topic is finished?* Not the content facts! Not the vocabulary words! What is the organizing idea that frames the topic?

When you determine this big idea that you want students to have when they leave your classroom, then this idea frames the conceptual understanding that you want to build on throughout your unit. Is this an easy task? No! When we started working with teachers and we asked them to undertake this task, one teacher after much effort said that he had narrowed the number of important concepts down to sixty-four! Thinking that this might be a little too many, we were able to negotiate the final number down to two. How do we get started on identifying the big ideas?

The first step is to stand back from the textbook or kit that you are using and examine your own understanding of the topic—not what the textbook or teacher's guide tells you, but your own understanding. It may be helpful to talk with others (for example, a teaching colleague, a friend, or a family member) about your ideas in relation to the topic that you want students to take with them. Many times, we begin by writing our ideas and creating our own concept map. Then, go to the reference material and check your understanding. We say the word *understanding* here because these are the ideas that you apply to a range of different situations; these are not the textbook definitions. This is what you have as *your* understanding. We have to be able to view the topic or unit as a concept framework with a central core idea(s); otherwise we struggle to implement cognitively based strategies.

> **HAVE A GO!**
> **EXAMINING CONCEPTUAL FRAMEWORKS**
>
> If you are going to implement these cognitive strategies you will need to begin with your own conceptual framework of a topic. Appendix E provides guidance for developing a concept map of a topic that you teach.

What does this look like? Next we have provided two examples, one from biology, the other from physics, to show you what we mean by the big idea of a topic.

## Example 1—Life Science

A topic that is included in most school curricula is ecosystems. Teachers need to ensure that students are exposed to a range of different biomes. Students need to understand that different biomes exist—tundra, rain forest, taiga, and the like—and that each of these systems has to deal with biotic and abiotic factors. Nutrient and energy cycles need to be dealt with in each of these different biomes. Is there a single common concept that links these knowledge points and ideas together? When the student leaves your classroom, what is the concept that you want him or her to have? An organizing concept for students to understand is that *any ecosystem is a changing system in which balance is maintained*. All the different biomes to be studied have the same basic structural features—decomposers, producers, and consumers—with abiotic factors cycling through each. Regardless of the biome these things exist, and all biomes are attempting to maintain a balanced system.

"Yeah, but this is obvious . . ." If it is so obvious, why are most textbooks not oriented around this idea? Why do teachers insist on treating the different biomes as distinctly separate from each other? They are separate in the types of plants and animals that exist in them, but conceptually they are all the same.

## Example 2—Physical Science

Topics covered in physics at school include magnetic, gravitational, and electrical forces. These are often covered in separate chapters and are not seen as being connected. However, they are linked by the single idea that the *attractive force between objects decreases with distance*. Yes, the origins of the forces—magnetic, gravitational, and electrical—are different; however, as distance increases, the effect of the force decreases. They all have the same basic equation:

$$F = \frac{Gm_1m_2}{d^2} \quad F = \frac{Kq_1q_2}{d^2} \quad \frac{F}{1} = \frac{kI_1I_3}{d}$$

The important concept for students is that regardless of the type of field being viewed, the force decreases. Students can then organize their understanding around the big idea and see that each of the examples studied has its own unique properties, but they are each linked via the organizing framework.

Having determined the big idea for the unit, teachers and students can now create a concept map that relates all the content of the unit in the manner in which it is connected to the big idea. The concept map will be a representation of how the knowledge of the topic is stored in long-term memory. The big idea becomes the organizing frame for all the content associated with the concepts of the unit.

A unifying idea or ideas exist within each of the topics being studied within a school. Teachers have indicated to us that defining this unifying idea is the singular most difficult task to do in planning a unit. We have tended to view learning as a linear path: If we lay out the pathway for the students, they will follow. Then, somehow at the end of the unit, having carefully laid out the "perfect" path for students, poof!—magically the conceptual view of the world will be unveiled and that is when the aha moment arrives. As teachers (sadly) in this scenario and view of teaching, we have not dealt with the conceptual framework of the topic, so that magical moment rarely occurs. Instead we have focused on the content, and thus reversing this pattern requires a different approach. We need to ask ourselves, what is it that we understand about the topic and how does this match up with theory on teaching and learning?

Thinking about a topic conceptually is different from normal practice and thus is more difficult. It does take some time. The concepts are not laid out very well in the majority of textbooks. How strong is my (the teacher) understanding of the topic? How easy is it for me to draw up a concept map of the topic? Our encouragement is to try this exercise; it is harder than it appears. What is (are) the major idea(s) that you want your students to leave your room with concerning the unit you are about to teach? What is the major idea that they can take with them no matter where they are and be able to use it? Try this task with a topic that you are familiar with so that you have a greater chance of succeeding. We believe this task is necessary because the evidence shows we have not been very successful with a vocabulary list as well as a list of content items in getting students to transfer these to new learning situations.

Why is it important to get the big idea(s)? If we are going to align our teaching with how we learn and what we know about how people learn, then it is important for us to focus on the concepts that frame a topic. If knowledge is stored as a conceptual frame, then teaching needs to be about helping students construct a framework consistent with that of scientists. If learning is about the negotiation of meaning, then students need to engage in the negotiation of concepts—in essence, they need to be constantly engaged in the act of negotiating.

Students who lack success in science, that is, who tend to score poorly, fail to come to terms with the language of science. A major problem is that they are unable to play the memory games associated with answering multiple-choice questions, fill-in-the-blank questions, or other such types of questions. By changing the focus to the big idea(s) of the topic, we are able to provide these students with an opportunity to change from the memory game to building an understanding of a topic. Students move a list of disconnected vocabulary words to negotiating meaning of the words in relation to the big ideas of the topic.

A critical component of student-centered learning strategies within science classrooms is for students to be engaged with scientific argument as a means to negotiate meaning. Students need to construct arguments and debate about the big ideas of the topic as central elements in the negotiation process. By working through claims, evidence, and warrants for a topic, the students will be able to move past a simple list of words to construct rich justifications for their understandings of the topic.

## Planning the Topic

The focus on big ideas does cause a change in how we plan a topic. Planning is not about how many pages in the textbook need to be covered in a single lesson or period, but how can the lessons be structured so that they help students build connections

# From the Students

In the example in Figure 3.2, we see how a student negotiates meaning through using writing in a creative form to explain her new science knowledge to an authentic audience: a parent. She mixes science vocabulary with rhetorical language to reach her audience while continually having to negotiate between what she now understands and how she can represent that in written form.

**Figure 3.2.** *A student explains the states of matter in a letter to her mother*

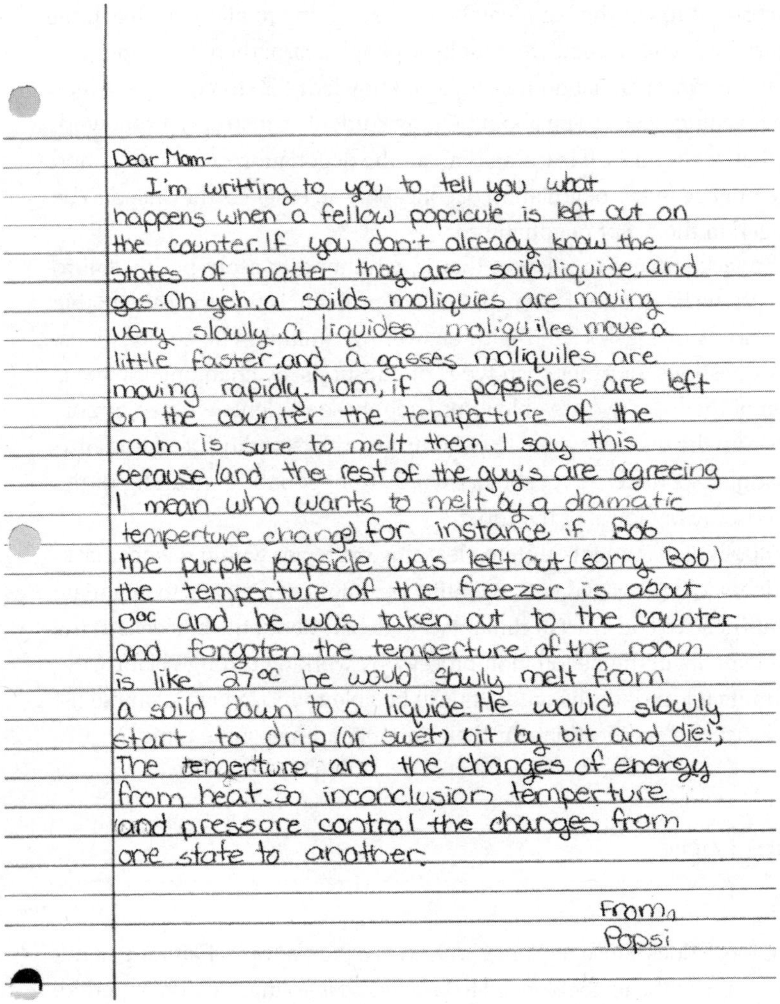

> Dear Mom-
>   I'm writing to you to tell you what happens when a fellow popsicule is left out on the counter. If you don't already know the states of matter they are soild, liquide, and gas. Oh yeh, a soilds moliquies are moving very slowly, a liquides moliquiles move a little faster, and a gasses moliquiles are moving rapidly. Mom, if a popsicles' are left on the counter the temperature of the room is sure to melt them. I say this because, (and the rest of the guy's are agreeing, I mean who wants to melt) by a dramatic temperature change. For instance if Bob the purple popsicle was left out (sorry Bob) the temperture of the freezer is about $0^{oc}$ and he was taken out to the counter and forgoten the temperature of the room is like $27^{oc}$ he would slowly melt from a soild down to a liquide. He would slowly start to drip (or sweat) bit by bit and die! The temerture and the changes of energy from heat. So inconclusion temperture and pressore control the changes from one state to another.
>
>                                   From,
>                                   Popsi

to the big ideas. Does that mean that there is a need to throw out all the activities that you have previously used? No! Does that mean that the textbook is not to be used? No! It does mean, however, that we have to take a different orientation toward this material. *Remember, we are not focusing on what we know*, we are focusing on how to help students build understanding. It is not a case of us as the teacher giving the information to the students so that they can give it back to us (this effectively means that we are really testing how much we know!). If we are going to implement inquiry-based strategies within our classroom, we need to have students active in the exploration and evaluation of ideas.

The first step in planning is to determine how many activities you believe are able to focus on the big ideas of the topic. Consider whether you are using the activity to demonstrate theory or as an opportunity for students to construct knowledge from the activity. Traditionally, we have used laboratory activities either as a means to demonstrate the knowledge that we have covered in previous lessons or to set up for coverage of material for the next series of lessons. The question that needs to be asked is how this activity promotes investigation of the big ideas. If students were able to pose questions about the activity, would they be able to derive claims and evidence from the activity that would help them construct an understanding of the big idea? How many activities do we need? This will be determined by how students respond to the activity. If they grapple with and understand the big ideas quickly, then the number of activities will not be great. However, as they struggle, more opportunities for engaging with the big ideas will be needed. *There is no set formula for determining the number of activities to be used.*

## Teacher's Voice

Thinking about activities aligned with the big ideas—this idea is a critical piece to the entire SWH process. Too often, as educators, we have students perform tasks because *we* enjoy them, not taking into consideration the merit and value that the activity has for learning. When I first began the process, I sought assistance with this aspect of the SWH. It was challenging to find activities that aligned with the big idea. It was next to impossible to make sure that the activities were inquiry-based. I found that collaborating with others in search of quality activities that aligned with the big ideas was a necessary step in the change process.

Having selected a series of activities that you want to incorporate in the unit plan, the next question is how to reshape these activities to promote student-centered engagement. Remember, *we as teachers do not control what goes on inside a learner's head—we control the learning environment.* Thus, we need to reorganize the activities to provide opportunities for students to pose questions about the ideas associated with the activity, complete the experience, and use scientific argumentation strategies to justify their conclusions.

Examples of change could include:

1. Not providing the blank shell of the data table to be used. How do we get students to understand what observations to do or what data to collect if we constantly provide fill-in-the-blank activities? Students should be working though what data to collect and how best to represent these data.

2. Require small-group discussion of the activity and posing of questions before they are able to undertake the activity. Rather than telling them what to do when and how to complete the activity, students need to wrestle with trying to understand what the activity is asking of them.

3. Helping students understand the nature of testable and researchable questions so that they are better able to refine their questions for further investigation.

4. Instead of groups doing exactly the same quantities, provide opportunities for variation of the quantities, examples, and the like. When the whole class is discussing the results, they will have to think more broadly and look for patterns. Students will have to account for variations and provide strong justification for the generalization being constructed. They cannot simply have the answer confirmed by the teacher.

In terms of planning the unit we have to be flexible. While we may plan ahead what we as the teacher believe is the most important sequence, this sequence may not be the one that the learners want to undertake. *We must remain flexible in our planning.* In the process of continually negotiating meaning with students, the appropriateness of the sequence that you have planned may need to change. What you have planned may not challenge or build on where the students have taken you. This does not mean that the activities you have chosen are not valuable; it means that you do not solely determine the sequence of their use as the teacher. In planning for the unit and then working through planning for individual lessons when teaching the unit, we must always ask the question, how will the activity support the students constructing understanding of the big idea?

Does this mean that we cannot give students information? No! If students reach a stage of not having knowledge of the activity or concepts being explored then we need to provide them with some information. We can, and need to, build in opportunities for information sharing with the students. However, unlike traditional forms of science teaching we cannot simply keep giving information—it has not worked well for us before, so why would it be any more successful than previous efforts? Thus, when planning information-sharing sessions it is essential that opportunities be built in for students to make connections between the new information and the big ideas of the unit. Remember, students will be trying to negotiate their understanding of what is being said. *We as teachers need to plan opportunities for public negotiation between new information and the big ideas.* As teachers we need to know what the students are doing with the new information. How are they connecting what we have shared with them to what they currently believe about the topic? Just because we give information does not mean that students will store the information in the manner in which we intended.

Having planned for activities and information sharing throughout the unit we also need to plan for some form of activity that will enable students to pull together all of the big idea(s) and content knowledge. This does not mean that they should copy the vocabulary list from the end of the chapter or the bold words throughout the chapter or complete the fill-in-the-blanks concept map. In all of our research projects, we have worked with teachers to use some form of a writing-to-learn activity as an end-of-unit summary activity. As will be discussed in the next chapter, writing-to-learn activities require students to move past "recall" knowledge to explain what they understand to different audiences using different types of writing. These activities might include writing letters to local government, writing textbook explanations to younger students, or writing brochures for the local tourist industry. This summary-writing activity is not simply an exercise in giving students practice at using the correct words; it is a learning activity as powerful as any of the others discussed earlier. As teachers we need to plan some form of activity that *requires students to summarize their understanding through the negotiated meaning-making process of writing.*

The final and critical piece of the planning process is the assessment component. By constantly engaging students in the negotiation of meaning we will be able to continually assess their learning throughout the unit. The question then becomes, how do we construct end-of-unit assessment? There are many ways to do this, including writing opportunities (we will explore this in the next chapter), practical activities, and tests. We would like to focus on tests as these are common throughout all schools; end-of-unit tests are the predominate mode of assessment. Traditionally, most tests are based around multiple-choice questions, fill-in-the-blanks, matching words, or algorithmic problems for which there has been lots of practice in class time. How are these types of questions focusing on students' understanding? Most of the questions that are traditionally used are about recall knowledge, that is, students are playing memory games. If we are trying to align our teaching to how we believe learning occurs, should we not be trying to align our assessment to learning? If the focus of our teaching is to have students build a conceptual understanding of the topic through the negotiation of meaning, should we as teachers not provide forms of assessment that require students to display that same kind of thinking? Why would we want to use assessment items that require only recall (low-level thinking) when we have been focused on requiring students to be cognitively active in constructing knowledge, that is, requiring them to use high levels of thinking? *Thus, when planning for assessment we as teachers need to match assessment to learning.*

## Teacher's Voice

One area I feel I still need to improve on is making assessment match conceptual learning. I was used to using fact-based tests. Attempting to write a concept-based test is difficult. I constantly question if I am doing it correctly. At times, students are frustrated with the test because it is something they are not used to doing. They are used to only skimming the surface. SWH forces them to dig deeper. I see evidence of this all the time during class discussion and activities. However, it does not always carry over to the test. I feel that if I work more on helping students learn to write to express conceptual understanding, they will improve on the end-of-unit test.

In all of our research projects, when working with teachers we have taken the approach of including extended-response questions on the end-of-unit tests. These questions require students to connect to real-world situations, to explain to other people certain components of the big ideas, or to display how the content knowledge is connected to the big idea(s) of the topic. These are not questions for which they have practice. As we will discuss in the following chapters, students in our approach rarely ever do end-of-chapter summaries and end-of-chapter questions from the textbook. While we have heard from many teachers that they always do this type of testing, all the teachers in our research projects have struggled with this facet of the teaching approach. Constructing these assessment questions take practice, both in framing the question and deciding how to grade or comment on the question. Remember, it is not only about the exact answer—the question is also about the thinking that the students display. Several examples of conceptual test questions are displayed in Figure 3.3.

## Find Out What the Students Know

After the planning, what is the next step? If we believe that learning is done by the individual and the individual constructs knowledge for himself or herself, then the starting point of any teaching-learning activity has to be the students. Thus the question becomes, how does what we as the teacher have planned fit with what the stu-

**Figure 3.3.** *Conceptual test question samples*

Earth Science
> Big Idea: The Earth is part of a larger system.
> Question: How is the Earth part of a larger system?

Biology:
> Big Idea: Cell structure relates to a cell's function.
> Question: If a cell were a city, what functions of a city would each cell part fulfill?

Physical Science:
> Big Idea: A force is a push or a pull.
> Question: Identify all of the forces acting on a cart rolling down a ramp and describe them. Draw the forces into the diagram below.

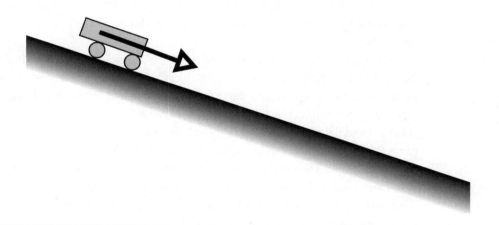

dents will construct? What assumptions do we make about students' existing knowledge?

We have heard and been involved with educators who tell us about aiming for the middle group of students in the class, to make sure all our goals and objectives for the lesson are clearly laid out, and to have our questions planned out. All this preparation work is about us, the teacher: We need to make sure we are prepared, ready, and able to complete our job of teaching. Where do the students fit in? Are they empty vessels for us to fill? Are they eagerly waiting for us to pass on the message? Where does learning fit into the act of teaching? Traditional science teaching would appear to treat these two entities, that is, teaching and learning, as two separate commodities. We as teachers teach; the students' job is to learn.

We need to see that learning and teaching are not separate acts and, thus, we need to conceptually link our teaching with how we believe learning occurs. Thus, we need to find out what students know before we start the unit. If we are going to help students build an understanding of a topic, we need to know what they understand at the beginning of the topic. It is not about what we know, it is about what the student knows. It is not about what students can recall or if they can complete the algorithms they have learned from the information we have passed on to them. Rather, it is about how we can assist them in building an understanding that they can take with them and apply wherever they are.

The first act of teaching for a new topic or unit is to create an activity that enables you as the teacher to find out what the students know. Wide ranges of activities can be used; for example, generating a concept map at the start of a unit is one way to explore students' initial understanding of the topic. We have had students read newspaper articles and debate a topic as a starting point. It does not matter what activity is used, provided it gives students the opportunity to voice what they know about the topic.

Having obtained this knowledge, what do we as teachers do? How do we use the plan that we have started to build? Remember that planning was about deciding the activities to be used and the content needed to address the big idea(s) of the topic. *The sequence of these activities and material occurs after we have found out what the students know, not before.* Teaching is about helping students build an understanding of the topic; it is not about us as teachers hearing the students parrot back to us what we already know. Thus, if we begin to have some understanding of where the students are, we can shape the sequence of activities so that students are constantly challenged and required to negotiate understanding. This is not easy to do—it requires experience at attempting to do this sort of planning. The plan will change for each section or class that you are teaching and will change every time you repeat the unit. We do not have the same students in each section. This does not mean that the plan will be radically different; it means that we have to be flexible enough to match the sequence of activities to the group of students that make up each section or class.

## Teacher's Voice

One tool we are using to get at what the kids already know about the topic is a pretest. The pretest is based on what we think are the main ideas and concepts that we want students to get from this unit. In the past, we were teaching from the book, and this is what the book says, this is the worksheet that goes with it, this is the lab that goes with it, or whatever. So, I think we are just more prepared in the beginning because we understand the major concepts and the big idea. Before there were too many concepts; now we are narrowing them down and saying, this is major idea—how are we going to approach it? How will we get at what the students know, and then, where do we go from there to get at the big ideas?

## Questioning

The previous sections relate to the planning of the unit. The emphasis on planning can never be overstated. Learning occurs when the plan is put into action—actually interacting with the students. Putting the plan into action requires two critical teaching skills: questioning and group work. However, a major caveat must be addressed. *A focus on learning requires good management strategies*; traditional, didactic, information-transfer strategies are centered on maintaining classroom discipline. In this form of teaching, management comes first and learning is a potential by-product. However, we see a need to separate management from learning and teaching. As teachers we need to ensure our classroom is safe, students are respectful and well behaved, and the environment is conducive to learning. This is not about teaching and learning. This is about *creating an environment that enables students to be involved in activities that are aligned to how they learn*. Having created what has been termed a nonthreatening learning environment, we can now implement teaching strategies that are focused on how we believe learning occurs.

We all question students—that is what we do in our classrooms every day. The difference about questioning if we adopt student-centered learning strategies is twofold. The first is that we can no longer play "guess what is in my head" games. Students are used to these games. They see us as teachers searching for the right answer, searching for the correct words. Having found the right words, phrases, or algorithm, we immediately move on—once we have the correct answer that is in our heads, then we assume that everyone else has the same idea and we can move on to the next question. We are taught to use the IRE (initiate-respond-evaluate) method: teacher initiates a question, the student responds with an answer, and the teacher evaluates the answer (Cazden, 2001). Then we wonder why students in our classes are reluctant to answer questions. Why should students put themselves up for exposure when they constantly lose in the game of "guess what is in the teacher's head"?

If playing games is not the way to go, then what is? Student-centered learning strategies are not about students guessing what is in the teacher's head, *but rather the teacher finding out what is in the students' heads*. If learning is about negotiating meaning, then questioning is a critical element of that process. We need to use questioning as a strategy to find out what is in students' heads, challenge their ideas, and debate the outcomes of the students' inquiry activities. We have to retrain the students to make public their reasoning strategies and how they have constructed their arguments.

What are some of the essential skills that we need to use? First and foremost, we need to get out of the way. We talk far too much. When we ask teachers to view videotapes of their teaching, they are horrified about how little time is spent in giving students a voice. In most cases we should try to pose questions that require students to move beyond recall and think through possible solutions to arrive at an answer. When students answer the question, two things have to happen: We have to stop making judgments about the answer, that is, we have to stop letting the students believe that we are the arbitrator for deciding whether or not the response is correct. One way of doing this is to constantly ask the question "Why?" every time a student responds. Watch the dynamic in the classroom change. Second, to encourage dialogue, we need to allow the group to pass judgment on the answer. Instead of you the teacher passing judgment, the class should participate and come to consensus. Some suggestions to support this process in the classroom:

1. Write down some questions about the topic you will be teaching tomorrow. Write down questions that will make students think. It takes time to move away from what we have always used.

2. To begin changing your questioning strategies, tell the students that for today you are trying something new and you are not allowed to give answers to questions. Every time you ask a question, ask another student to pass judgment, for example, "Mary, is John's answer OK? Why?"

3. What if the students agree to an incorrect answer? Then you as the teacher need to pose a question that will challenge the answer. For example, you may comment, "I understand the answer you put forward about X, but I was wondering what would happen if I did Y?" Remember, your simply telling them the answer has not worked in the past. Change to their ideas occurs because the students make the change, not because we want or tell them to.

4. Give the students time to talk through possible answers with their colleagues. For example, "Turn to your partner and decide on an answer and a reason for your

answer—I will give you two minutes." Then you can seek the groups that have the same answer or different answers and ask them to explain their reasoning.

The important point to remember when questioning is that you are trying to determine what is in the students' heads and why they have arrived at these ideas. Negotiating meaning is not about passing on information; it is about challenging students to account for their ideas and maneuvering them toward the scientifically acceptable ideas.

Does this mean that we cannot ask recall questions? No, of course we can. However, these types of questions should not be the predominant mode of instruction. Even when asking these questions, still ask other students to confirm the answer. It takes time and practice to change our habits, and thus we need to continually spend time practicing these different techniques.

## Teacher's Voice

Well, you know, I think that learning to question just takes practice. I am not great at it by any means, but I think you just learn to wait and then think about their responses. You have to continue on in that direction—what else can we ask them or how do we get the other students involved? What do they know? Do they agree or disagree? What do you think about that? You have to get them involved and that gives more time to develop questions to think about. But I really think the knowledge of the content, which we all have, will allow you to develop questions. I think it is just the matter of changing. It is more of changing your style and being better at it. We were all asking questions before, but I think we are doing more now. And try to have them be more meaningful.

We often hear people tell us that they have been doing inquiry teaching for many years. When we dig a little deeper, what they mean is that they have their students doing activities, activities that are set by the teacher, with the direction of the questions being controlled by the teacher, and "guess what is in my head" games being the dominant questioning format. We will keep coming back to the idea that *we have to change what has been our traditional mode of operation. We need to choose some simple starting point and practice.* Watch the change in your students. They will resist the fact that you are not going to supply the answer. They will complain that you are not doing your job. However, what does become obvious quickly is that the quiet students tend to find a voice because now they do not have to fear being wrong. The low-achieving students who do not play the memory game well can now become involved because the questions are not about right or wrong but about the big ideas. The dynamic of the classroom will change.

Another area of change that we need to have when talking about questioning is dealing with the situation of information sharing, that is, when students have arrived at an impasse and we need to provide information—often called just-in-time instruction. Direct information-sharing teaching occurs just when the students require it. Traditionally, we seek to ask questions that confirm for us that the students have the information that we have transmitted to them. We use the IRE pattern of questioning, searching for the correct answer. As soon as we have the answer—generally from the students who always answer correctly—we move on to the next point that we want to make sure that they understand. We often ask the question, "Does everyone understand X?" Nobody says anything to the contrary and thus we assume that they all know it. We know that not all the students understand, and even if they answered that they were unsure, what would we do? Would we repeat our explanation or try to find a better explanation? The important idea that we need to keep in mind is that it is the students who are going to make the connection between what they know and what you have told them. Our questioning needs to challenge them to explain how they are connecting the bits of information. Thus the simple question becomes, how is what we have just talked about connected to what we have been dealing with through the activities of this unit? Again the strategies discussed earlier need to be put into action. Ask students to discuss with each other what they think or ask students to compare each other's answers—any strategy that requires them to explain how things are connected.

There is no one set of questions that we can ask to achieve success. There is no predetermined series of questions that have been found to be better than another for us to learn for success. What we always tell teachers is that as professional teachers you need to build questioning strategies that work for you in challenging students' understanding. We need to constantly remember when questioning students in our classroom the overarching question that we must ask ourselves: Whose knowledge am I dealing with by asking this question? By stepping away from simply telling and playing "what is in my head" games, we can change the dynamics of the classroom into a nonthreatening learning environment where all students can engage in the subject matter.

## Teacher's Voice

The change process and breaking the habit: The way you instruct in your classroom is a habit. For many of us, when things get rough, we go back to our old habits. Changing the way you teach science will be no different. This process is not a new curriculum; it's a new philosophy. It's a different way to think, believe, and act. Change is not easy. Do not think for one second that you can read this book and then go into the classroom and exhibit quality, inquiry-based instruction. All parts of the process are critical to the SWH being effective. However, the most difficult part for me was the questioning methodology. I had grown so accustomed to being the "almighty beholder of knowledge." We played the "guess what is in the teacher's head" game frequently in my classroom. My level of questioning was also very low according to Bloom's taxonomy.

When attempting to incorporate the inquiry questioning techniques, I found myself constantly affirming or denying the student responses. This was my bad habit. Forcing myself to let go of the reins and allow students to truly think and affirm or deny one another through the power of debate meant giving up ownership. To make this paradigm shift in your teaching, I would strongly recommend videotaping and self-assessing your questioning strategies. Equally beneficial would be the use of a peer coach. Having someone within your team or department going through this change process gives you an encourager, a motivator, and someone you can have professional dialogue with. In time, the techniques will get better. It simply takes practice. Remember, this process is not about changing what you teach; it's a philosophical change in how you teach.

## Group Work

We believe that implementing group work in the classroom is critical for success in student-centered learning environments. Students need to be provided opportunities to negotiate meaning across different settings—individual, small group, and whole class. The reason for providing these different settings is that a critical component of negotiating is engaging in public understanding of the ideas. An individual student does not live in isolation from his or her peers, family, or friends. Students are constantly moving between different social groupings where they have to give their thoughts, opinions, and beliefs. Such activities are part of their daily lives. However, in science classrooms we rarely give them opportunities to discuss, debate, and construct arguments for their ideas. Students are engaged in individual negotiation of meaning the whole time. All the time that they are sitting in the classroom, not saying much, they are constantly trying to work out how what they are being told fits into what they already know. The problem is that they rarely get a chance to have a voice in explaining what is going on and how they have put the pieces together. If we as teachers constantly ask questions that have only one acceptable answer, then individual negotiation by students is never challenged.

The function of group work is to promote the shift from individual and private negotiation of meaning to public negotiation of meaning. We want students to put their ideas out there to be challenged by their peers. Students will change their ideas more readily by this process than by us telling them that they are wrong. Of course we have the "yeah, buts . . .", "some kids don't like to talk," or "they will not stay on task." Try this exercise: at the end of the lesson with five minutes to go, stop teaching. Pretend to be getting something and do not comment about the noise or talk. We guarantee that all the students (or nearly all) will be involved in a conversation. Why? Because they can talk and they are talking about what interests them. So, we can establish that all kids like to talk. In addition, not one of the students was off task in talking to each other. What we have to do is to focus the conversation so that they are discussing something that is about what they know. Throughout this chapter we have been talking about big ideas and questioning students about these during the course of the unit. The intent is for us to engage the students' ideas, to value their thinking, and to assist them to build scientifically acceptable understandings of the concepts. Group work is critical in this process.

Small-group work is where students can be engaged in laboratory-type activities, debate information shared by the teacher, argue about solutions to problems, frame alternative explanations, and attempt to reach consensus. Small-group work is where students who are reluctant to speak in whole-class settings can have their voice heard. Thus, the activities done in these small groups should be focused on the students exploring their own ideas.

The teacher needs to take a number of important pedagogical actions with small-group work:

1. Explore different ways to set up the small groups. These range from normal friendship groups, to random drawing of names out of a hat, to purposeful selection by you as the teacher.

2. Make careful decisions about how long you keep the same arrangements of students together. Do not be frightened to change the grouping arrangements every now and then.

3. As teachers we need to monitor the conversation occurring in the groups and work out how close the ideas are to the big ideas of the topic. The questions we pose will be around challenging the students' concepts and how closely they match to the big ideas for the topic.

4. Monitor the time that you have students in small groups. This can be centered on when you see that all groups have completed discussions or the set task. This skill gets better with practice. It is important not only to keep the flow of the classroom going but also to allow the students enough time to have meaningful opportunities to engage with what is being asked of them.

5. Remember that when groups are working, your role is to challenge their thinking. When interacting with groups it is important that you do not give answers to the students unless the questions are procedural. We need to have

the students understand that you are going to challenge them and that the intent of the exercise is for them to determine the answers.

6. Have mechanisms and strategies in place for all groups to have their ideas or answers in the public view. For example, each group has to put their ideas on the board or on a large piece of paper to be hung up. Remember, the intent is for the small group's negotiated position to be further negotiated across the whole class.

There is no one correct way on how to run small groups. As teachers you have to blend your own style with means to promote opportunities for students to build knowledge. Group work is essential—thus, *you as a teacher need to explore what particular strategies you will use to set up, monitor, and challenge the groups.* It can be very difficult for us as teachers to stop talking, to stop trying to pass on all the knowledge, and to let the students have control of the learning process. Two important points: One, we as teachers have never had control of the knowledge inside the students' heads, and second, small-group work is an ideal, nonthreatening way for all students to be involved in working with their own ideas. *Remember, individuals control their own learning process and teachers structure the learning environment.*

The transition between small-group and whole-class discussion is important. One of the major problems the teachers who we work with have had is in adjusting their pedagogical actions when dealing with these two different situations. Most teachers are comfortable when they practice with small-group work. However, they are much more uncomfortable when trying to do the same thing at the whole-class setting. The difficult part with whole-class settings is trying to continue with the concept of challenging students' thinking when you have twenty-five or thirty students rather than four or five in a small group. A critical strategy builds on Point 6, discussed earlier. As a teacher, what strategies do you have to examine the small-group outcomes that are different from the traditional teacher-centered, teacher-controlled whole-class discussions? How do you help the whole class come to a consensus about the ideas they have been discussing? How do you make sure that the students' ideas are aligned with the scientifically accepted ideas?

One of the difficult tasks with whole-class work is the need to balance where you as the teacher need to get in terms of the curriculum and where the students are at in their understanding. If we can continue to involve the students in a conversation about the concepts, then we can help them make the change. For example, when discussing a particular phenomenon students will use everyday language. Remember, we cannot simply tell them what the science word is—we need to enter negotiation by saying such things, "Instead of using the word $X$ scientists use the word $Y$. Is it OK if we use the word $Y$ from now on?" The students generally say yes, and thus you can begin to use the correct terminology in a manner in which the students

## From the Students

On this board, the students have stated their claims related to their rocket-building experience. Then, as a group-negotiated process, they organize their claims under the big headings of Weight and Weight Placement, Forces on Rockets, and Nose Cones. The students created the categories after a whole-group negotiation examining the patterns in the claims that they were making individually and in small groups (as written on the sticky notes).

**Figure 3.4.** *Students negotiated responses to the study of forces while they were creating rockets*

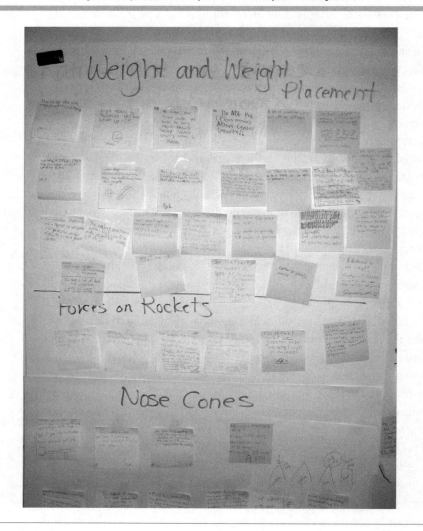

can attach meaning to it. Instead of short-term memory games, the students can build conceptual understanding and meaning that will be stored in long-term memory. Another example when working with whole-class settings is to generate some conclusions as a class without referring to the textbook. Having reached consensus, then ask the students to check the textbook to see how what they have come with up matches what the scientists say. If you have managed to steer the questioning and information giving to the right answer, the students will be comfortable with the answer. If there is a mismatch between their answers and the scientifically acceptable answer, you can immediately instigate a discussion. Again, this discussion will provide opportunities for the students to negotiate their own meaning.

The difficult part of whole-group work is that we as teachers struggle with the dynamics that can and will occur with the lively discussions that can result. This is a critical element in moving to inquiry-based approaches; when we struggle with the discussions we tend to retreat to our traditional didactic approach and the students, seeing the old "guess what is in my head" games, will retreat away from the discussions. It does take time to become skilled at these types of conversations, but never getting started means never trying. We have all fallen on our proverbial faces—it does not mean we have to retreat. By setting up a nonthreatening learning environment where everyone gets a chance to talk and all answers are valued, then the dynamic in the classroom will change. Even though you have the answer that you wanted very early in the conversation, challenge the students. Do not let them know they have arrived at the answer—test the confidence they have in the answer. It is when they as a group can make choices about the concepts that their understanding will grow. It is easier to do this in small groups, but as teachers we need to keep working on this in the whole-class setting.

### HAVE A GO! MANAGEMENT VS. TEACHING

We often confuse classroom management with teaching. Management is an important component of your work, but it is not teaching based on what we are claiming here. Have a go by writing out what you do during your day and then identify each task as either teaching or management. Go to Appendix F and compare your list to further examine teaching and management.

## Revisiting the Big Idea

Matching teaching to our views of learning means that we have to change some of the strategies that we use in our classrooms. In this chapter, we have tried to provide some background to what we think are the essential skills that as teachers we need to employ when using the SWH approach. We recognize that while some of these skills may be familiar, they do change depending on how you view learning. The purposes involved in the various skills change as a consequence of focusing on the learning. It does change what happens in the classroom, the type of environment that you create, and the support that you receive from the students. We need to change how we question students, how we use group work, and how much control we think we have of student learning. Our encouragement is to keep trying—work on one particular aspect, and you can see other parts of the teaching and learning dynamic changing also.

# CHAPTER 4

# Writing in the Science Classroom

A s science teachers we all know that writing in the science classroom is a necessary undertaking for all students. It is important that they are able to get notes from the board into their books, are able to record data during their laboratory work, prepare and complete laboratory reports, and answer test questions. We would agree with you that these activities are important for students to be engaged with during science inquiry. However, we have also heard over and over from science teachers that we are *not* English teachers and thus it is not our responsibility to deal with it.

Our response to this statement is to ask the teachers to teach their next science lesson without any form of language—text language, mathematical language, pictorial language, graphical language, or symbolic language. Think about how easy that task would be—*without language there is no science.* There is no means of doing science, understanding science, or communicating about science without language. Language is fundamental to science because we need it to do science and build further on what we know, that is, to be practicing scientists and derive new knowledge; we need language (Norris & Phillips, 2003). So rather than sticking our heads in the sand and pretending that language is not important, we need to recognize that language is important for science and explore how we can incorporate opportunities within our classrooms to allow students to build a better understanding of science through engaging in language activities.

Much debate currently exists in the research field about how to best use writing within classrooms. Two major views oppose each other. These can be characterized as learning how to use language and using language to learn.

# Learning How to Use Language

Many researchers have suggested that for success in science, students must learn the language patterns of science before they engage in the practices of scientists. Most of the activities that students are involved with are performed prior to actually doing the science. Examples of this view include the following:

1. Students must learn to practice writing up a laboratory report as a critical function of science. They need to know what the laboratory report structure is and how scientists use it.

2. We need to ensure that students have a vocabulary list of words prior to working on a topic so that they can recognize the terms in the textbook. This list is to be given to students prior to beginning the topic.

3. We need to teach the students about scientific argument separate to doing science, that is, we need to teach them about the structure of argument separate to inquiry so that they can argue about the topic.

We refer to this position as a mechanistic position—the students need to learn the mechanics of the language. While a number of research studies have been conducted to determine the value of this particular position, the results are inconclusive (Klein, 1999).

# Using Language to Learn

The opposite position to the one discussed in the previous section is that students learn through using the language, that is, the language is introduced to them as a part of being involved in science lessons. Language practices become embedded within the science lessons as a means to help students construct understanding. Examples of this view follow:

1. Having completed a laboratory activity, students explore the structure of a report in order to present their findings and conclusions to the teacher.

2. Students are introduced to science terminology when there is a need for the term—terms are introduced when needed so that students can build connections to their meaning.

**3.** Scientific argumentation patterns are part of the laboratory activities. Students are introduced to argument as a consequence of having to discuss, debate, and defend their results and conclusions.

We refer to this as the "language to learn" position, that is, students can learn about the language as a result of using the language. While there have not been a large number of studies that have explored this position in science classrooms the results to date have been positive in terms of helping students learn science (see reference list at the end of the book and in Chapter 10 for a variety of articles on this developing research).

## Which View or Position Should We Use?

*We believe that we should use language as a learning tool.* Building on the work of theorists such as Gee (1996) and Lemke (1990), we believe that students will have much greater connections to science and the language of science if they can build from what they know. Students need to have a purpose to engage in the language practices of scientists—simply to have to do it because it is important for the topic is not motivation enough for students. We need to create reasons for students to have to engage in using the language of science. Students are voting with their feet; they do not go on to science careers because they cannot connect to science. They do not see the purpose of engaging with science.

The language to learn movement is more aligned with learning as described in Chapter 2 than is a more mechanistic view of learning language. If we allow students to use what they know as the beginning point of using language then we engage with what they know, not what is external to them. If the understanding of the science and the language is built within the context of science, then student confidence in both the science and language grows.

Our research has focused on the use of writing-to-learn strategies within science classrooms. Thus, most of the discussion will be focused on this area, although we will weave in opportunities for reading and talking as the opportunity arises.

## What Is Happening When Students Are Writing?

A number of different theories are used to try to explain how we learn when we write about a topic. These theories recognize that simply asking students to recall information is not a writing-to-learn experience. That is, asking students to list the

## From the Students

Look carefully at the following example from a student engaged in an SWH experience about energy forms. What is she able to show us that she knows about energy? How is language a learning tool for her to explore her understanding? Is she simply reporting knowledge or in her writing is she demonstrating that she is still thinking and negotiating what she knows and how she can explain this so it makes sense not only to herself but to also the audience for her book?

**Figure 4.1.** *Writing samples from a student engaged in an SWH experience*

**Figure 4.1.** *(Continued)*

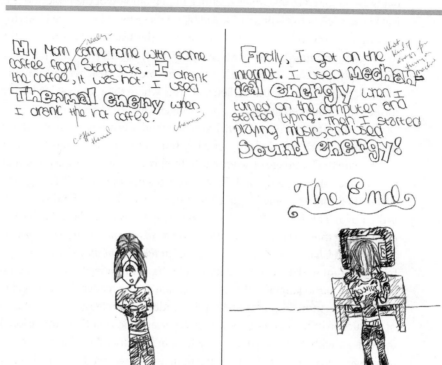

parts of a flower or to write down the first twenty elements of the periodic table are simply recall tasks and are not viewed as learning tasks. However, when writing is viewed as a learning task, the differences between the theories are essentially revolving around the idea that when someone undertakes a writing task in science they have to use two knowledge bases: the science content knowledge base and the rhetorical (language) knowledge base.

When we ask students to complete a writing task that requires them to explain a concept to their peers, present an argument to a younger audience about the science-related ideas of a topic, or write a newspaper article to inform an audience, then we are asking them to move past recall of information. Asking students to take what they know and reframe it in a different form means that their knowledge is transformed (Berieter & Scardamalia, 1987) or constituted (Galbraith, 1997) in a new way. The students are required to take their scientific understanding of the topic and their rhetorical knowledge of the writing task and blend these two knowledge bases together. By moving the audience for the task away from the teacher, the students have to pay much more attention to the words that they use to describe the science. No longer can they simply give back to the teacher the "big words" the teacher gave them; they have to break these down for the audience. This is where their knowledge becomes transformed or constituted in a richer and stronger way.

It is important to remember that when students are writing about a topic for a different audience, they are engaging in a number of different translations. They have to translate the language of science into their own form of language so that they can understand what is being said. Remember, science language is foreign to your students; therefore, the only language that they have to understand what is being said is their own. This is why they fall back on using the big words of science without understanding them. *Having them learn lists of words means that they can spout back to you a list—a label. It does not mean they know what the term means.* However, when writing for a different audience, the students now have to translate what they understand about the topic to language that is appropriate for the reader. These acts of translation become even more important when the students' own language is not the language of instruction or the language of science. This task adds another dimension that needs to be dealt with on a daily basis. Teachers must remember that science is a unique language—it is not part of common language and we need to provide opportunities for students to use it and build connections to it.

Returning back to Chapter 2, we know that learning is about negotiating meaning. When we are writing for different audiences or for ourselves in ways that require more than recall, we are negotiating meaning. Through the act of writing we have to negotiate meaning between our own language and science language. The written product is about science but constructed through the perspective of the learner. If the student's first language is not the language of instruction, then an added translation occurs: home language, school language, and science language. This step is not trivial—the complexity of the negotiation is both difficult and important in helping to build understanding of the science concepts.

The arguments for reading and talking are the same basic arguments about negotiating meaning. Reading is about trying to negotiate meaning from the text that is presented to you as the reader. Reading this now you are trying to negotiate meaning between what you know and what we as authors are trying to relay to you. The same is applied to talking. Debate, argument, and discussion are attempts to negotiate between the people in the conversation.

## From the Students

**Figure 4.2.** *A fifth-grade student shares her understanding of biomes by creating a travel brochure, thus representing her science knowledge in a new form, to a different audience, using a variety of modes (words and pictures) to explain her new understanding*

*continues on next page*

**Figure 4.2.** *(Continued)*

## Landforms

If you like to go rock climbing or canoeing then the Grand Canyon and Colorado River are what your looking for. Enjoy a hike on a trail on the Grand Canyon go canoeing on the Colorado River and stay at the "It Isn't too Hot Here Inn," located in the Sonoran Desert.

| # of people | 1 person | 3 people |
|---|---|---|
| Cost | $25.00 | $75.00 |

Give us a call at 536-2810

Max. people per room 6
Hotel includes:
1 indoor swimming pool
1 lobby
1 kitchen
air conditioning

## Plants/Animal/Insects

Come see the world's largest cacti, the Saguaro and Cardon. Some trees you'll see there are the Joshua tree, the Mesquite tree, and the Agave tree. Some animals that live there are the Cactus Wren, Gila monster, Side Winder, Spadefoot toad, Ant-lion, Harvester Ant and the Jewel Wasp.

Cactus Wren

Saguaro          Mesquite tree

**Figure 4.2.** *(Continued)*

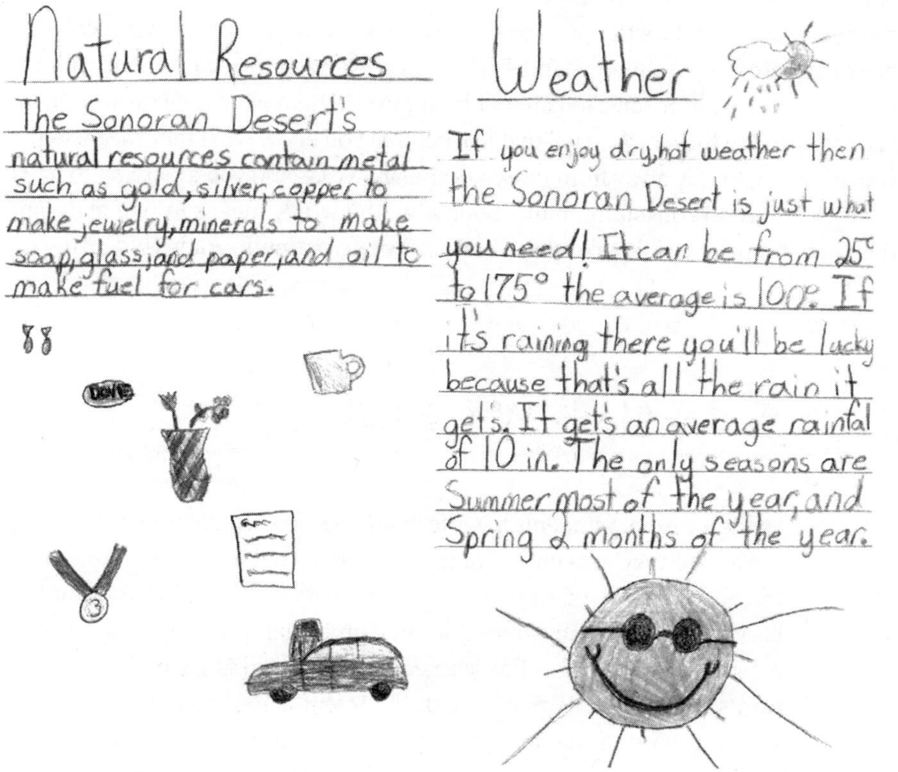

# Natural Resources

The Sonoran Desert's natural resources contain metal such as gold, silver, copper to make jewelry, minerals to make soap, glass, and paper, and oil to make fuel for cars.

# Weather

If you enjoy dry, hot weather then the Sonoran Desert is just what you need! It can be from 25° to 175° the average is 100°. If it's raining there you'll be lucky because that's all the rain it gets. It gets an average rainfall of 10 in. The only seasons are Summer most of the year, and Spring 2 months of the year.

## Setting Up the Writing Task

While we expect students to write within our science classrooms we have to ask ourselves, are they actually learning anything from this task? For example, notes from the board are copied so that students have a record of what you want them to give back to you to demonstrate that they understand the topic (we would argue that most often the student has learned the game and is giving back what the teacher wants to have learned). Although the intent is for the students to gain an understanding, written chapter summaries really focus on what is going to be on the test, and end-of-chapter questions are completed because these serve as practice test questions. While the extent of the argument here may be a little overstated, the question still remains: how often are the students given opportunities to use writing as a tool to explore their own understandings, to use writing as a learning tool?

Building on the comments earlier in this chapter, we believe that writing needs to be embedded within the context of the science-related activities. It should not be seen as something that is outside of science itself—it is more than just a recording device. Remember, there is no science if there is no language. To move beyond the use of writing as a mechanical approach to a learning tool view, we need to consider what the conditions are that will help students construct meaning from its use. Writing for most people is not an easy chore; it requires hard work because it is cognitively demanding. If you haven't done some writing that required explaining something to a nonteacher audience lately, try writing a letter to parents explaining your teaching and learning philosophy without using educational jargon. Sit down and begin to craft a letter. How many drafts do you think it will require to get a finished product that is clear and conveys meaning in a language that can be understood by your audience?

In recognizing that this is a difficult task, what are the strategies that we have to use to help students? There have been some studies conducted (Rivard & Straw, 2000; Hand, Hohenshell, & Prain, 2004) that have begun to examine some of the necessary conditions for helping students use writing as a learning tool. These studies show that students need to be involved in a planned approach that incorporates opportunities for talking, reading, and drafting. We believe that the following are critical components that teachers need to address:

1. **Big ideas.** Students need to focus on writing about the ideas that frame the topic. If writing is going to be used as a learning tool, then the writing should be about the concepts that frame the topic. The students need to negotiate through the writing experience what their understandings of the topic are. The very act of writing will help them shape what it is they think they understand.

2. **Small-group discussion.** Students need opportunities to discuss the ideas that are to be addressed in their writing with their peers. This initial discussion provides opportunities for students to have a more risk-free environment to discuss, defend, debate, and negotiate their ideas. The students need to put some collective ideas together that they can present to the class for feedback.

3. **Whole-class discussion.** Students need to have opportunities for their outcomes from the small-group discussion session to be presented to the class as a whole. This creates opportunities for further public negotiation of meaning. In this phase, the students have to be critical consumers of the work put forward by peers. The feedback the students receive needs to come from the class. Some of the feedback can be related to the appropriateness of the language to be used for the audience, such as, "Are the big ideas clear?"

4. **Further small-group discussion.** This presents an opportunity for the small group to assess the whole-class feedback and readdress any changes that they think are critical for the audience.

5. **Production of first draft.** Students are required to produce their first draft individually so that it can be given to the audience for evaluation. We believe that the students should write to a real audience and that the audience needs to be involved in the process.

## From the Students

In this example, a student uses multiple forms of representation to display his message and his negotiated understanding about the states of matter. He uses text and visual images to display his thinking to an audience of his peers.

**Figure 4.3.** *A cartoon created by a student studying the states of matter*

6. Production of final draft. After receiving feedback from the audience students should be given an opportunity to redraft their first attempt. This step will allow them to respond to the comments from their readers in terms of both the language and science content.

While we have written this as a list of points, we are presenting the optimum set of conditions. As teachers you will frame the task to best suit your classroom. However, we would emphasize that you provide the maximum opportunities for student negotiation to occur.

The next question is how to choose the appropriate writing task for the students. We believe there are five key components for a writing task. These are topic, task, purpose, audience, and method of text production.

# Choosing a Writing Task

When beginning to think about what type of task you want the students to complete, consider the criteria mentioned in the previous section: topic, type, purpose, audience, and method of text production. Each of these is discussed below:

*Topic.* As a teacher, you need to be clear about what it is you want the students to write about. We have focused carefully on ensuring that students are required to deal with the concepts or big ideas of the topic. We believe that the benefits of writing are centered on building conceptual understanding, that it provides opportunities for the writer to link together the major connecting ideas of the topic. Thus, teachers must carefully consider both framing the teaching of the topic, as outlined in Chapters 2 and 3, and helping the students build their conceptual understandings.

*Type.* We have placed emphasis on trying to diversify the types of writing used in science classrooms. Traditional writing tasks include chapter summaries, notes from the board, occasional posters, and laboratory reports. We believe that students ought to be asked to write in ways that provide greater opportunities for engagement in meaningful writing tasks. Thus, we have asked students to write newspaper articles, letters to the editors, letters to younger children, textbook explanations for younger children or peers, and poetry.

*Purpose.* In using writing-to-learn strategies we believe the purpose of the writing tasks needs to be more than recall of information or memory tasks. Writing can be used at different times throughout a unit or topic, and this will change the purpose of the topic. Writing tasks can be completed at the beginning of the unit to explore prior understandings of the topic; this can be used as the jumping-off point for the unit. During the unit, writing can be used to consolidate knowledge being constructed. End-of-unit writing can be used to persuade, explain, or argue to different audiences as a means to construct rich understandings of the topic or unit. These are just some of the purposes that writing can be used for at each stage of the unit: beginning, during, and end of the unit. As a teacher you can be determine the particular purpose. However, we would encourage each of you to move beyond the purpose of recall.

**From the Students**

**Figure 4.4.** *Fifth-grade students write poetry about their new understandings about freshwater and marine water*

Fresh Water
Clear, Rough
Flowing, Splashing, Mixing
Currents, High Tides, Low Tides, Estuary
Twisting, Spinning, Fast Moving
Still, Swampy
Marine Water

Fresh Water
Beautiful, Clear
Flowing, Dripping, Dropping
Ecosystem, Animals, Plants, Pressure
Turning, Swaying, Twisting
Gorgeous, Smooth
Marine Water

*Audience.* As we have discussed previously, we must move beyond the traditional audience of the teacher to gain benefit from the use of writing-to-learn strategies. Our research has shown that students can most benefit when writing to younger audiences, peers, or the general public. These audiences require the need for translation of science language into everyday forms of language. Our interviews of students have indicated that if students have to write to teachers or older audiences, they do not focus on translation. In fact, just the opposite—they tend to want to use the big words of science because they believe they are expected to show what they know.

*Method of text production.* This criterium is about how the students construct their text. Do they do it individually? Do they work in groups? Is the product to be handwritten? Computer-based? These are questions that you as the teacher need to make in relation to the writing experience. As suggested earlier, you need to provide small-group and whole-group discussions prior to the production of the final text to support the students in getting a better understanding of the expectations of their audience.

## Assessing Student Writing

One of the difficulties for science teachers is how to assess the writing that students produce. As we often hear, we are teachers of science not English, and thus, we should not be worried about our students' writing skills. In what we have been talking about so far, we have emphasized the need for students to be able to negotiate meaning through talking, reading, and writing—do we need to assess all these elements? The answer for us is "No"; we focus on trying to assess the writing that the students produce.

However, we do need to address what is to be assessed. If we are going to ask students to write for different audiences, for different purposes, using different writing types than they normally use, then we need to assess them in a different manner. Students must be assessed on the science concepts being addressed and on their efforts in fulfilling the rhetorical or language components of the task. Decisions about how best to do this need to be based on what reporting system you use in your setting—marks or descriptive feedback. Either way, determine the criteria that you feel best suit your situation. Points of consideration for criteria:

1. Big ideas. If the unit is based on big ideas, then students must be able to show understanding of these concepts.

2. Writing type. Has the student successfully laid out the piece of writing in the format that was required (for example, a letter, a textbook explanation)?

# From the Students

**Figure 4.5.** *Two examples of letters students wrote, one from one body system to another, to demonstrate understanding of how the body systems work together to support one another*

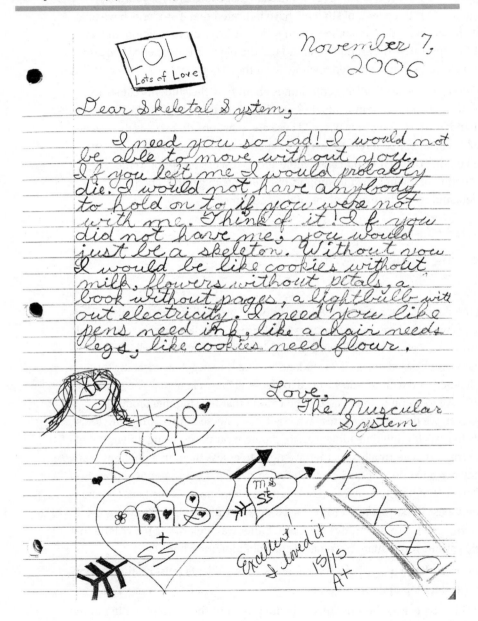

LOL
Lots of Love

November 7, 2006

Dear Skeletal System,

I need you so bad! I would not be able to move without you. If you left me I would probably die. I would not have anybody to hold on to if you were not with me. Think of it! If you did not have me, you would just be a skeleton. Without you I would be like cookies without milk, flowers without petals, a book without pages, a lightbulb without electricity. I need you like pens need ink, like a chair needs legs, like cookies need flour.

Love,
The Muscular System

Excellent! I loved it! 15/15 A+

**Figure 4.5.** *(Continued)*

November 9, 2004

Dear Mom and Dad,

As you know, we have been studying rats and nutrition in science. We had a test rat named Cheeto and a control rat named Melon. We fed the test rat junk food and the control rat healthy food. Every week Tayler and I had jobs. The first week we got their food and the third week we cleand their cage.

The control rat gained a lot of weight. The test rat gained a little weight. When the project was over the control rat was biger than the test rat. We found that out every Friday Over every week the control rat grew abou 30g and the test rat grew about 10g. The reason is because the test rat got less calcium than the control rat.

I learned that dew to lack of calcium you can get osteoporosis. Your spine can bend , you can grow weak and you can die and if you drink enough milk you can prevent these things. My favorite part was cleaning the cage.

Love,

**3.** Audience. Is the writing appropriate for the audience (the only way to test this is to get the audience to evaluate the writing)?

**4.** Flow. Does the writing flow, are all the terms clearly explained for the audience, is the spelling correct, are paragraphs formatted, and the like?

If you have to use letter grades for assessment, then decide carefully what you believe are the most important elements. For example, when we work with teachers they generally begin by placing most of the marks on the science concepts. However, they quickly understand that they must recognize the rhetorical demands placed on the students and adjust their distribution of marks accordingly for the next assignment. If you do not need to give out marks, you can use a descriptive scale such as "in need of improvement" to "good effort."

A critical element of assessment for us is the audience—we involve the audience in assessing the student products. We provide the audience with the same scoring matrix that the teacher is going to use because we believe that it is absolutely critical that the students have to write to a real audience and the real audience has to be involved in the feedback and assessment. Otherwise, the students quickly realize that they are really writing only for the teacher and fall back into not explaining the science words.

Does the audience truly review the work of peers? We have explained to tenth-grade students that they need to ensure that they pay attention to what they are writing to their seventh-grade audience. They become a little shocked when the seventh-grade student responses are brutal and honest about the quality of the work that they had to read. It is a powerful lesson for students to understand that writing to an audience does involve paying careful attention to what and how you explain the concepts being discussed. We often encourage and provide opportunities for students to redraft their initial attempt and then these are given back to the same reviewer. Once the audience has reviewed the written product the teacher also assesses the product. Interestingly, we find a strong correlation between the audience review and the teacher's assessment.

An important consideration for us is that we provide the scoring matrix for the students before they start the writing task. We believe that this helps the students orient to the task and understand the aspects that are important to consider when engaging in the writing process. More examples of assessment tools will be shared in the next chapter.

## Revisiting the Big Idea

In this chapter, we have tried to provide some background to what we think are the essential language and writing skills that as teachers we need to use with the SWH approach. We recognize that while some of these may be familiar, they do change depending on how you view learning and how you organize writing opportunities in your classroom. The purposes involved in the various writing skills change as a consequence of focusing on the learning and with consideration to topic, type, purpose, audience, and the method of text production. Assessing this writing is also an important consideration, but with a reminder of who controls learning, it is essential to include the student in this assessment process by allowing the audience for the writing to provide key feedback and assessment in addition to the teacher.

# Examining the Science Writing Heuristic Approach

With the theory laid out in the first four chapters, it is now time to examine closely the components of the SWH and how these components lead to a learning approach that puts teaching into the service of learning. The next chapters break down the SWH approach into the parts that make up the whole learning experience.

We often talk about the SWH as a "lens" through which to take a look or a new perspective on your science teaching and the learning of your students. It is not a tool kit of strategies but rather a way of thinking based on the theory and philosophy of learning that you just read and experienced in the first section of this book. Now it is time to delve into the SWH process. Get ready to dig deeper into your own teaching and learning experiences. Put the book down and walk away when frustrated, but keep thinking and processing. As you argue and wrestle with these ideas, listen to your students and ask them to join you in this process of examining teaching in the service of learning.

### HAVE A GO!

Professional development often produces a less-than-positive response in teachers. Often we are forced into the current required meeting sessions that usually wouldn't be what you would choose to do with your time. Section I is very theoretical and hopefully made you think about teaching and learning in deeper, fresher, and unique ways. Have a go at describing what you would want in a professional development program in Appendix G.

In this section, we will take you through the SWH process:

❖ Getting started with your first SWH unit in Chapter 5

❖ Learning to use Questions, Claims, and Evidence in Chapter 6

❖ Using Reading and Reflection to energize thinking in Chapter 7

❖ Wrapping up a unit with the summary-writing experience in Chapter 8

# Getting Started with the SWH Approach

Teacher's Voice

One teacher's thoughts: I really want to examine the beginning of the whole process. I'd like to give up the ownership of providing the kids the guided inquiry. I used to go that way to be safe so that we could focus on what I thought would be more valuable. I really want to get the students mature enough to be able to start right off the bat with their own questions.

The first four chapters have set the foundation needed for transitioning to a learner-centered classroom where teaching shifts to focus on learning. When considering the changes necessary to implement the SWH approach effectively it could be easy to view the SWH-related learning processes as only slightly different from what has traditionally happened in science classrooms. However, nothing could be further from the truth. The orientation of the classroom, planning, questioning, and management take on radically altered forms in such a setting. In an SWH research study, a student in anonymous interviews commented on her view of the change in classroom culture prompted by the SWH process (see the "From the Students" below).

---

### From the Students

I don't like the SWH. Before, I was always the top student. I know how to play the game and score well on tests. Now the rules have changed. It isn't about playing the game, it is about learning, and I have to work just like everyone else. Just memorizing doesn't work anymore and I have to work at this.

---

The next three chapters will guide you through the implementation of the SWH approach from start to finish. But make no mistake: The changes called for in this text are difficult to achieve and will necessitate honest self-assessment about your own content knowledge and teaching practices, the learning environment you create in your classroom, and your beliefs about learning and teaching. This is not your traditional science class, it is not your traditional science teaching, and it is not your traditional science learning. This is a process that builds from what students already know to a conceptual understanding of the big ideas of science. Let's take a look in this chapter at the following questions:

1. What is the SWH?

2. Why should I use the SWH?

3. How do I start using the SWH?

## What Is the SWH?

The Science Writing Heuristic is an approach used in science classrooms that actively encourages students to negotiate meaning both privately and publically, creating a learning environment that is rich in opportunities for argumentation and learning. The process uses argumentation as the center where learners must build a conceptual understanding of whatever concepts are being studied and defend their ideas in a public setting. Sound familiar? It should. This is the process of science. Scientists explore their questions and must defend their ideas about answers with their colleagues and the scientific community.

While the SWH approach can be seen as a series of templates, teacher, and students, it is much greater than that. The resemblance to a traditional lab write-up is superficial. The approach reaches across curricular areas and incorporates language, reasoning, argumentation, and critical thinking. In the primary and elementary grades the opportunity exists for the SWH approach to reach across all classroom activities, whereas in the secondary classroom the teacher has to be oriented to make those connections and opportunities. Developing these connections is a critical component to the approach, and finding other faculty that will make those connections with you enhances the science learning. For the connecting faculty, this approach will also strengthen student reasoning, literacy, numeracy, and the elusive but continually sought-after critical thinking.

The actual heuristic is a structure that helps students develop a deeper understanding of the big ideas of science. When considered in its entirety, students develop and test questions, justify their claims with evidence, compare their ideas with others, and consider how their ideas have changed throughout the process. At the conclusion of a series of SWH experiences focused on big ideas of science, students write about their learning not only to communicate with others but also in the spirit of a writing-to-learn experience.

# Unit Planning Using the Science Writing Heuristic (SWH)

The graphic in Figure 5.1 represents the structure that forms the foundation for the SWH experience. Notice the unit is planned around a big idea of science; the first thing that happens in the classroom with students is the assessment of their prior knowledge. As students move through the process, they engage in a series of SWH activities, with each experience generating questions to guide the next. The final step in the process involves a summary-writing experience.

The framework in Figure 5.2 outlines the SWH process that guides students to examine their thinking and test their ideas as they move throughout the unit. While seven steps are listed to steer students through the learning process, the order and flow may be altered to meet student learning needs. Remember that the learner is in control of his or her learning and the process should align with the students' learning needs. The open nature of the circles in the model in Figure 5.1 is meant to represent this flexibility.

The SWH in Figure 5.3 allowed the students to explore the problem and put their claims and evidence down on paper. Even though the claim is faulty, it will move the learning forward. With questions and just-in-time teaching the teacher can use this SWH experience to move learners forward and help them construct a more accurate understanding of the big idea here. Teachers often will tell students the correct answer. Providing correct answers doesn't make students correct their conceptual framework to match the teacher's conceptualization. Incorporating new information into a student's conceptual framework isn't that easy, and you as teacher providing information probably isn't enough to produce a shift in learning. If students are at the point of frustration, providing information to keep them engaged is warranted at appropriate times, but the information-provider model of teaching doesn't align with the SWH approach.

In this case the teacher chose to tell the students that they were wrong, but a simple question in the process would have been powerful. "Aren't these times basically the same? Is the mass making a difference?" These questions, asked either by teacher or other students, are part of the negotiation process and the construction of meaning.

## SWH Tool

The large circle represents the unit. The big idea is the beginning point for the unit and the rest of the process flows from that big idea. Student understandings of the big ideas are assessed and then the unit flows from that assessment through the SWH experiences and a summary-writing experience leading to the final assessment.

**Figure 5.1.** *Graphic representation of the flow of an SWH unit*

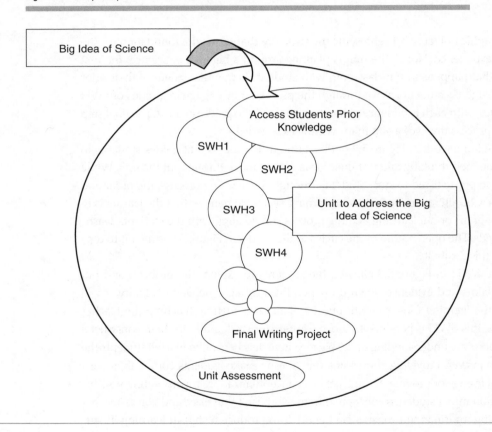

**Figure 5.2.** *The SWH framework for student use during investigations*

---

## The Science Writing Heuristic

Name _____

1. Beginning Ideas: What questions do I have?

2. Tests: What did I do? (How did you test to answer your questions?)

3. Observations: What did I find? (What did you find when you tested?)

4. Claims: What inferences can I make? (Explain what you think happened.)

*continues on next page*

---

Figure 5.2. *(Continued)*

## The Science Writing Heuristic

Name _____

5. Evidence: How do I know? (Justify your claims by providing evidence for them.)

6. Reading: How do my ideas compare with those of others?

7. Reflection: How have my ideas changed?

# Why Should I Use the SWH?

The SWH is a process that is consistent with what research tells us about learning and effective teaching. The SWH approach brings together inquiry, reading-to-learn strategies, writing-to-learn strategies, and classroom discourse into an intentional and student-centered process for developing understanding of the big ideas of science.

The evidence of the impact of the effective implementation of the SWH approach on student learning has been very encouraging. The effective implementation of the SWH increases all students' conceptual understanding of the big ideas of science as measured using student responses to open-ended questions and increases the achievement of all students on standardized assessments. Even more significant is how the effective implementation of the SWH approach closes the achievement gap—it has a greater impact on traditionally low-achieving students. For more details, see Chapter 10.

## From the Students

The following student work sample is from an SWH-focused pendulum motion addressing the big idea that the acceleration of the object is not a factor of mass. Note how the student recorded questions and described the tests and observations using a combination of common language and scientific vocabulary. The student constructed a claim and then supported the claim with evidence. In the reading section, there is no indication of the source(s) and the student reported that his or her ideas compared with the class but were wrong. The students worked through the process and their prior conceptions influenced their claims and evidence. The times for all masses as noted by the teacher are nearly the same, yet the student claim indicates that the mass makes a difference in the energy and the evidence is the comparisons of time. This SWH allowed the teachers to really see the class's conception of acceleration due to gravity. Also note that the sample shows evidence of scoring by the teacher.

*continues on next page*

Figure 5.3. *Student example of the SWH process*

Science Writing Heuristic Template

Name_____

Hour _Period 5_____

Date _11/13/02_____

**Science Writing Heuristic Lab:** _____

1. **Beginning ideas…** What questions do I have?

   How does to

   How does energy cause motion?

   3
   3
   3
   3
   M
   ———
   +19

2. **Tests…** What did I do? (How did you test to answer your questions?)

   We swung the pendulum to see how long it took for it to swing back and forth 10 times. and We kept adding more weight. Our string was one meter long and we dropped the weight from table height.

3. **Observations…** What did I find? (What did you find when you tested?")  10 swinger

   100g - 20.47 sec = 0.49 sw/p/s          20.47 sec
   200g - 20.59 sec = 0.49 sw/p/s    ⎫ actually
   300g - 20.38 sec = 0.49 sw/p/s    ⎬ all pretty much the same.
   400g - 20.70 sec = 0.48 sw/p/s    ⎭ As we know gravity causes all
                                           mass to accelerate same
                                           rate.

**Figure 5.3.** *(Continued)*

| 4. Claims…What inferences can i make? (Explain what you think happened.) |
|---|
| The More Mass the less energy you have and the less Mass the More energy you have. |

| 5. Evidence…How do I know? (Justify your claims by providing evidence for claims.) |
|---|
| I think this because when 100g was on the pendulum it swung 10 times in 20.47 sec and when 400g was on the pendulum it swung 10 times in 20.70 sec. |

| 6. Reading…How do my ideas compare with others? |
|---|
| when we compared with other people we all agreed on the same claim but it was wrong |

| 7. Reflection…How have my ideas changed? |
|---|
| I learned the More Mass the More energy and the less Mass the less energy. |

## Teacher's Voice

From my perspective, we have been working hard to develop an inquiry approach to our science curriculum and we lacked the means to effectively evaluate and write up the lab experience. The traditional lab write-up was inadequate. From the SWH experience, I saw much more investment on the students' part in the inquiry process. They understood that they were writing their thoughts down and they were keeping track of their questions and the tests they ran instead of me always assuming the students could hold that in their minds and then produce the final report or final work. So, I liked the SWH approach and the way students took an active view of work in progress, the heuristic format, journaling, and the writing that I saw taking place.

I think that manifested in the interviews. When I give students a lab and they follow Step 1, Step 2, Step 3, even if I encourage them to branch from there with their own technical question and their own experiments, they often asked "What are we doing this for? What are we supposed to learn from this? What does this have to do with the chapter?" Those would be the kinds of questions or comments. When the students were engaged in their own SWH process they knew what they were doing it for because they had ownership. They sought a link to acceleration that they understood. I know that took some teacher guidance and some scaffolding questions but they engaged because they owned the work— it was theirs, not mine.

The SWH approach also creates a pattern of reasoning that is embedded in a structure of argumentation. Learners in the SWH approach have two roles: construct knowledge and critique knowledge in the argumentation process (Ford, 2008). This approach is more than just the practice of knowledge construction in science. The roles learners engage in are the very foundation of reasoning, critical thinking, and engaging with new ideas and information. These roles within the approach are the basic building blocks of all knowledge construction, not just science.

## How Do I Start the SWH?

The SWH begins with you:

* your ideas about teaching and learning,
* the classroom environment you create with your students,
* the unit planning you do for the students.

Given the importance of beliefs about teaching and learning to the successful implementation of the SWH approach, think about how you have responded to the following questions related to the work you did in Appendix A, C, and D:

What is learning?

What is teaching?

How do you like to learn?

How do you like to teach?

You may have struggled with the complexity of these questions. As you consider your responses, examine whether there is a disconnect between how you like to learn and how your classroom is structured. Remember, you construct the learning environment, and your ideas about teaching and learning will impact whether and how well you implement the SWH approach. Your ideas about teaching and learning should align with how you structure your classroom in general and how you implement the SWH in particular. As you begin the process, work to align the classroom with the learning and teaching concepts you developed and strengthened in Section I.

> **HAVE A GO!**
> **WHAT DO YOU AND YOUR STUDENTS THINK ABOUT TEACHING AND LEARNING?**
>
> Your students are an important part of the SWH. As described earlier, effective use of the SWH approach requires a learner-centered classroom. To help set the stage for transitioning to a focus on learning, ask your students to get involved in the process and answer the questions above and in Appendix H.

Did you find their answers interesting? Some examples of student responses to these questions are listed in Figure 5.4.

How do these responses match your classroom? These answers indicate a very sophisticated understanding of how we "do school." Traditionally high-achieving students often are adept at describing a traditional model. Their success has been predicated upon their ability to understand that model and excel within that learning environment as voiced in Figure 5.4. When implementing the SWH approach, preparation is critical to a much greater degree than in traditional lesson planning because the teacher doesn't predetermine the learning path. Instead, the learning path is a product of individual learners, small groups of learners, and the class as a whole. If they choose a direction that wasn't anticipated or planned for it can be very disconcerting for the teacher. In this kind of learner-centered classroom, the teacher needs to be flexible while maintaining a focus on the intended learning goals framed by your student learning standards.

## From the Students

**Figure 5.4.** *Student answers to what is teaching and learning (generated by students who have not had SWH training)*

### #1: Explain what learning is and support it:

Learning is the gaining of knowledge of subjects. For example, a student learns from watching and listening to what a person says and does.

Learning is figuring out new things to help you in the future.

Learning is receiving knowledge not known before, such as learning how to draw an object to scale using proportions.

### #2: Explain what teaching is and support it:

Teaching is sharing the knowledge that was learned. For example, information is shared and given to students for the students to learn.

Teaching is passing on knowledge to someone else. For example, a teacher taught us how to draw an object to scale.

Teaching is imparting knowledge upon another individual.

Starting with a well-thought-out personal conceptual framework around the big idea will allow you to maintain flexibility and focus. Consider your own understanding of the content. A teacher concept map is an excellent place to start. The core of the content is based on your standards or grade-level expectations. You have a curriculum that you are responsible to teach that includes standards. This approach isn't asking you to change your curriculum, just how you teach and support your students' learning of that curriculum.

From there, your own concept map can provide a concrete guide to learning no matter where the students begin and no matter what learning path they choose to build their own understanding. In Figure 5.1 the process starts with assessing students' prior knowledge about the big ideas of the unit. A strong concept map that shows your understanding of how the ideas in the unit are connected provides a map for learning as well. When students reveal their prior knowledge on the topic, the map then can serve as a guide to you to help take them along the path of constructing a more complete understanding of the big ideas of your unit.

This also includes finding out what students already know about the concepts to be learned as a significant part of the planning. Students come to the classroom with lots of ideas—they have a conceptual framework that is built from prior experiences and knowledge—about the big ideas. We need to think about what these frameworks might look like before the unit begins in order to deal with the range of student ideas.

As you think about the various learning paths that might be chosen by students, you will also want to consider what is possible in your classroom with the available materials and equipment. You may choose to "seed" the questions that will likely be asked by putting equipment out on tables that could be used in an investigation into the big idea. You might also choose to set up a demonstration or stations to prompt student questions. Even with these prompts, students will choose their own paths. For example, they might test mass before speed, or pH before temperature, or surface area before weight. Your challenge is to consider the range of possibilities and be prepared to support students in finding the answers to their own questions.

Another challenge is to guide them through the use of scaffolding. Students may generate a question that involves many different variables. Help them think about where to start with their investigation. Some of the questions that they ask may be more easily researched than tested. In this case, you'll want to be prepared to help them find the experts or text resources to "investigate" or help them think outside the box and look for ways that they might build models or run tests with the available equipment. They may surprise you with their creativity.

Considering student learning standards raises the issue of "covering the curriculum." You as the teacher are required to cover your curriculum and likely "prepare" students to do well on standardized assessments. When using the SWH, the preparation looks different. Rather than focusing on covering facts and memorizing vocabulary, the focus is on the students' development of conceptual frameworks. This development will require students to examine their own thinking and test their ideas.

## Models of Unit Plans Using the SWH Approach

The following table shows alternatives used by four teachers as they used the SWH approach to teach a unit on ecosystems. The table represents the pathways the teachers followed through the process. Keep in mind, there is no one right way to do this. The following chart is meant to illustrate for you the multiple paths that a teacher can take to help individual learners develop the frameworks necessary to understand the big ideas of the unit.

## SWH Tool

**Figure 5.5.**  *Teacher pathways for ecosystems*

### Unit Concepts (or "Big Ideas")

| Unit Flow | Teacher 1 | Teacher 2 | Teacher 3 | Teacher 4 |
|---|---|---|---|---|
| Unit Planning | Teachers complete their own concept map | | | |
| Beginning point for unit | Teacher poses questions about topic | Teacher provides topic and students build concept map as individuals, in small groups, and as a whole group | Students work in small groups to research biomes and make presentations | Teacher provides the topic |
| Assessment of prior knowledge | Teacher to assess students' prior knowledge and gives pretest to assess prior knowledge | Concept maps are used to assess students' prior knowledge | Presentations used to assess prior knowledge | Student-generated questions and student dialogue are used to assess prior knowledge |
| Teacher planning | Adapting of activities and materials to student needs<br><br>The SWHs selected fit the student questions and the unit concepts | | | |
| Question generation | Student questions are based on what they want to know | Habitat study in the park using a transect technique is used as lead-in to students generating questions | Student questions are generated based on presentations | Students work in small groups and pose questions about the topic |

## SWH Tool

Figure 5.5. *(Continued)*

| Unit Flow | Teacher 1 | Teacher 2 | Teacher 3 | Teacher 4 |
|---|---|---|---|---|
| Multiple SWH activities emerge to address student questions | SWHs are varied based upon student questions; each student or group of students will do tests to answer their questions | SWHs are based on variation of the transect technique and questions are tested in park | SWHs are structured based on research in written materials to determine what is in an ecosystem | Teacher and students work together to plan tests based on student questions; SWHs are based on students' questions about balanced systems and habitat destruction |
| Summary-writing task | Students create a biome proposal and present it to peers; peers evaluate the proposal and accept or reject it based on student-generated criteria | Controversial topic: persuasive argument or position paper | Students respond to speculative questions (e.g., What will happen if . . .) | Public service announce-ment about ecosystems and habitat destruction |
| Unit Assessment | Unit assessment including conceptual questions | | | |

## Teacher's Voice

I think benefits of using the SWH approach include that it breaks the classroom out of a traditional model of teacher-to-student learning. Their world has now changed and it's not something that they have always done. This makes them approach their learning with a "new vision," so to speak. Also they have to invest some of themselves into the process, which is the difficult change for my students. Having to invest of themselves into their intellectual path as active participants who have questions or claims and evidence they had to defend in public with their peers was uncomfortable in the beginning. And the idea that they have to really build an argument and see if that argument will stand in comparison to classmates and their work is both threatening and satisfying. Our ideas are just that, our ideas, and we get a great deal of satisfaction when our ideas can stand on their own. I think those are the biggest issues. Some side issues are just the idea of you and your students negotiating your way through and fighting with each other to come to some kind meaning, or their egocentric hold onto their ideas or set of ideas and defending them until they either give up or see a better solution can create a classroom that is energized and students leave exhausted from the challenge of all this.

## Revisiting the Big Idea

To successfully implement the SWH approach, you must examine your beliefs about learning and teaching, content knowledge, teaching practices, and classroom environment with an emphasis on change. Planning is critical as you think about your own conceptual framework as well as consider the range of ideas students will bring to the classroom around the big idea to be addressed in the unit. The SWH is an iterative process that begins with a focus on a big idea of science, involves assessment of students' prior knowledge, helps students examine and test their ideas through multiple learning experiences, and ends with a summary-writing experience. The effective implementation of the SWH has yielded strong gains in learning as measured using student responses to open-ended questions as well as in student achievement on standardized tests.

Using the SWH approach means that you and your students will need to change the way that you "do school" in your classroom. Skills at classroom negotiation are critical to affecting this kind of change and the creation of a learner-centered classroom.

# CHAPTER 6

# Questions, Investigations, and Justifying Claims with Evidence

In the first section of this book, you had an opportunity to think about the differences between teaching, learning, and understanding as well as the relationships among these ideas. Key to these relationships is the idea that teachers provide learning opportunities, but only the learner controls what happens inside his or her own head. Even then, learning is only one step in the process, and our end goal is to help students construct an understanding of the big ideas of science in a way that is transferable from application in one situation to application in another situation.

As stated earlier, the SWH approach provides a way of planning for and scaffolding powerful learning experiences for students. To begin the process, students' prior knowledge is engaged by getting them to think about what they already know. Through the process, we teachers can assess students' prior knowledge as we consider what students bring to the unit investigations, where their understanding is incomplete, and where they have misconceptions.

Key to designing the kinds of learning opportunities that address students' current level of understanding is to engage students in asking, investigating, and ultimately answering questions. Through the process, students compare their ideas to the ideas of others using a variety of sources including their own classmates, as well as consider how their ideas have changed through the experience. Typically, at the conclusion of a series of SWH experiences that guide students into deeper understanding of their initial questions, they write for a specified audience about what they have learned. This writing opportunity serves as an authentic assessment of their learning.

As teachers, we create a learner-centered classroom by promoting classroom discourse and the negotiation of ideas. We must avoid the temptation to be the "answer-giver" or "explainer" and reinforce students' efforts to ask and ultimately answer their questions by making a claim and justifying it with evidence collected from their investigation. As discussed earlier, teacher answers don't change conceptual frameworks in students' heads. By creating experiences and asking probing questions, students are forced to address links in their frameworks that don't match what they are experiencing.

## Generating Questions

The first phase of the SWH approach is: *Beginning ideas: What questions do I have?* The process of asking questions is at the foundation of the SWH. This is important for both students and teachers because the root of learner interest is asking questions based on what the learner already knows and what the learner wants to find out. By reading this text, you are thinking of yourself as a learner. In that vein, think about a time in a class, meeting, or professional development experience when you felt no connection to the topic or had a question that you'd like to pursue but had been given no time to think about it or investigate it. You probably felt a sense of apathy, frustration, or perhaps even anger. Now imagine how the experience may have been different if you had been able to make a connection to the topic by asking questions and hearing the questions of others, and then been given the opportunity to pursue those questions relevant to you and others in the room. This image of learning becomes reality with the SWH approach.

### HAVE A GO! STUDENT QUESTIONS

People are naturally curious and want to find out the "why" of what they experience. However, in school we often don't see that human characteristic expressed in class. Have a go with your students to see if you can get them asking questions (see Appendix I).

The natural tendency of children is to ask "why" with every new concept they encounter. "School" may have squelched students' natural curiosity and wonderment about the world around them. Their desire to learn needs to be energized. One goal of the SWH is to reintroduce learners to the desire to learn all we can about the world around us. The trick is to make a connection between the science curriculum and what the learner wants to learn. To accomplish this requires learner investment and ownership.

Through the SWH, students have an opportunity to ask questions and hear the questions of others, pursue them through investigations and research, share their findings as they compare their ideas to the ideas of others, and consider how their thinking has changed through the process.

Accessing students' prior knowledge helps students make connections with the content of the curriculum and generate questions around the topic. As teachers, our challenge is to make decisions about which strategy is most effective for the particular topic as we begin the process of helping students generate questions. Concept mapping is one strategy frequently used by teachers to begin the process. Many other strategies for accessing prior knowledge are available, including:

❖ KWL

❖ Student-generated analogies or metaphors

❖ Teacher questions and classroom discussion

❖ Teacher demonstrations or demonstration stations

Strategies such as these can be used to introduce the unit or lesson topic and create opportunities for students to generate questions. Teachers have used the following four basic entry points into the process:

❖ Have students generate concept maps about the unit topic and then have students generate questions about the topic.

❖ Introduce the unit topic and have students generate questions about the unit topic.

❖ Introduce the lesson topic and have students generate questions about the lesson topic.

❖ Begin with an experience related to the unit topic, to help the students generate questions.

## Concept Maps

Research in learning (see Chapter 2) and our own experience tells us that accessing students' prior knowledge is the first step in helping students learn with deep understanding. With that in mind, begin the unit by generating your own concept map as described in Chapter 5. In constructing your own map your understanding of the unit's big ideas will become clear. The map will also serve as a guide to the unit learning. With a concept map in hand no matter where the students go, you have a map that will help you design and provide learning experiences that will move the learners toward a richer understanding of the concepts.

Having students construct concept maps about the unit topic helps uncover their prior knowledge. Through the process of constructing their maps and conversations about the topic, students identify what they already know or think they know about the topic. Based on their maps and their conversations, students generate questions about what they would like to know. You can use these maps as a valuable tool to guide your teaching based on the information that the students provide. In the SWH student example in the previous chapter, students had misconceptions about force of acceleration due to gravity with a pendulum. A concept map may have

# From the Students

Students write their ideas on sticky notes about motion and forces. The advantage of notes is that they can be moved to help organize ideas into groups.

**Figure 6.1.** *Motion and forces sticky-note board*

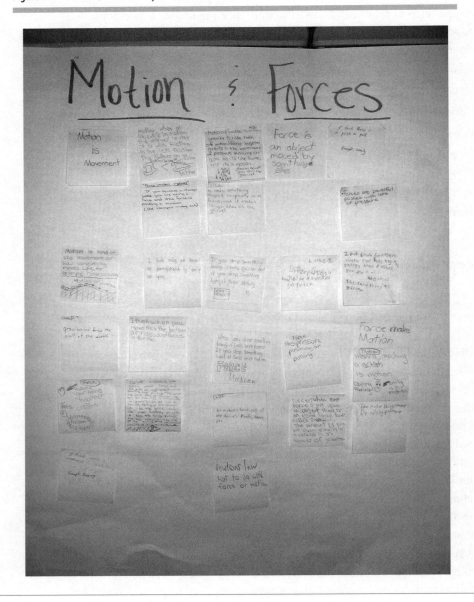

pointed out these misconceptions early in the unit and given guidance to the unit design.

In general, concept mapping is a strategy that can be used by individuals, small groups, or the entire class. When the SWH approach is new to both teachers and students, provide individual students time to think and get some ideas on paper, but generate maps in small groups and with the whole class. This method presents an opportunity to practice classroom discourse and promote the negotiation of ideas. Through the process, students build skills in working together and communicating their ideas more effectively. Building the concept maps in groups will also add to the pubic negotiation of meaning and the argumentation process. Your goal is to build an atmosphere in the classroom where all ideas must be scrutinized and stand on their merits. Imagine a classroom where the student who always "knows" the answer must defend his or her ideas against challenges from the quiet students. Teachers who use the SWH approach regularly report that students who have always been the ones that everyone looks to for the answer have faltered and not been able to support their ideas in the classroom discourse. The oral language nature of this process also enables students who have reading issues to engage using oral language.

## Teacher's Voice

The class was working in small groups and was trying to build concept maps based on the big ideas of biotechnology, specifically recombinant DNA technology. A student who was in the learning disability program because he was a nonreader stood up and said, "Wait a minute!" This student then proceeded to give a thorough and complete explanation of the concept that the groups were struggling with. The class was mesmerized and listened intently. When he was finished, his friend who was in his group said, "Wow, you've never talked in class before." At that moment the student realized what he had just done and had a sheepish look. He understood for the first time that he could learn just like his friends and that he was in charge of his learning.

Working together to generate a concept map also lends itself to the generation of "common" questions about the unit topic for further study as part of the SWH. This helps to limit the number of investigations that may be going on in the classroom at any one time and helps maintain a tighter focus on the learning goal. The concept map also serves as a guide as students begin to write about their understanding in later stages of the SWH. The development of common concept maps also offers another mode for collecting information about what students already know as you move around the classroom, listening to conversations. Both the process and the product help teachers identify challenges in student learning represented by incomplete student understanding or misconceptions. The concept maps provide the basis for students to identify areas of interest and to generate questions about the topic. The following scenario describes one teacher's experience with having students use concept maps to access prior knowledge and generate questions.

## Teacher's Voice

Concept Map Construction: In the ecosystem concept maps of students, it is quite possible that a student will identify a concept but have no idea how that concept fits into the big picture. He or she may know an ecosystem has physical and living components but cannot connect how these different components relate. This can lead to a question, and as teacher you can help identify the weakness or gaps in the student's understanding by simply asking questions as well as having other students asking questions about the concept map. The goal of the questioning would be to either help the student identify a clearer understanding than what he or she communicated or realize that the student doesn't really understand what is on the map, in which case he or she would come to the point of saying, "I really don't know. I wonder . . ." His or her wondering is the genesis of a question. After building a group concept map, have the students identify all the questions that came up during the map-building process. The class can then begin to identify the questions that will be most helpful in adding knowledge to their maps or to clarify their maps.

Regardless of who is generating the map, the goal should be the same. By focusing on students' prior knowledge, the concept map can be used as a graphic representation that leads students to identify the missing pieces of the map in the beginning of the SWH and generate questions to be tested or researched. In Figure 6.2 is a concept map that was generated by a group of students working on a forces and motion unit.

These maps demonstrate what a concept map might look like. The students have listed the topic for the SWH on their maps and then added their thoughts around the topic. Their maps were different but all were centered on the forces and how forces produce motion. The unit used rockets as the learning experience for the SWH. The students used their map to help them form their questions by graphically representing their existing conceptual framework and by looking for areas of the map where they weren't clear about their understanding. These areas were then used as a beginning point to generate their questions.

The concept map shown in Figure 6.2 shows the students' knowledge and how all the pieces fit together. The graphic includes the ideas in the bubbles, and on the connecting lines are words that show the relationship between the ideas. It is the

# From the Students

**Figure 6.2.** *Concept map for forces and motion*

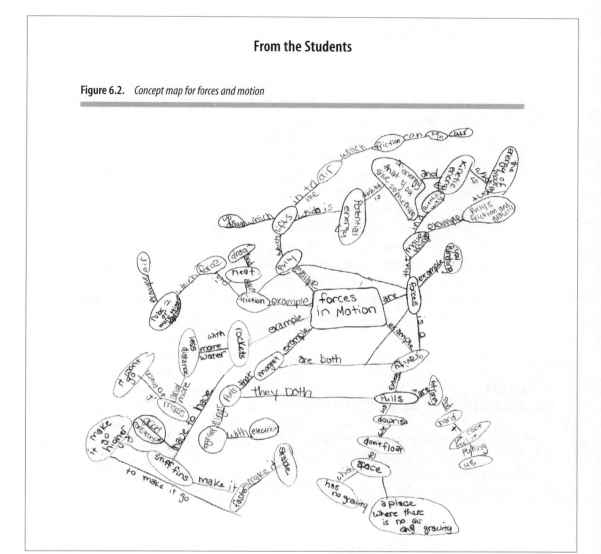

connecting words that show the relationship between all of the particulars in the scope of the map. Without these connecting words you have a semantic web, which doesn't show how the students think all of the particulars fit together into a big idea.

As students progress through the SWH experience, they can revisit their group's concept map as a way to monitor their own learning. They can add to, delete from, and modify the ideas represented on their concept map based on their new learning and emerging understanding. These are important steps in building ownership, self-monitoring, and becoming a better learner.

# Unit Questions

We know that student questions can be a powerful motivating factor and that the very nature of student questions can help teachers assess students' prior knowledge. With that in mind, some teachers begin the entire unit by having students generate questions that they have about the topic. Teachers begin by having students work individually and then in small groups, or by simply beginning in small groups to generate questions about the topic. Eventually these ideas are shared with the whole class. The student questions will be broad, and many of the ideas that are part of the curriculum will be represented in the students' ideas. The teacher can then help students focus on these questions for further study.

The teaching component of this process is critical. Skillful guidance through suggestive questions can lead the students to pick questions that are the most fruitful and match your curriculum. In the concept map presented in Figure 6.2, look at all the possibilities for a lesson direction to take and then think about guiding the class through questions that will enable you to meet your curriculum. If the lesson is about how unequal forces produce motion, it would be easy for the class to move easily down a trail of questioning about air pressure for launching the rockets. (In this lesson the class used air-powered rockets as the SWH learning experience.) If the class wanted to just increase pressure for launch, a question about the air pressure relationship to force could guide the group back to your curricular goals.

> **HAVE A GO!**
> **USING QUESTIONS TO GUIDE DISCUSSION**
>
> Go to Appendix J and have a go at using questions to move and guide a classroom discussion toward your curricular goals.

# Lesson Questions

When teachers are just beginning to use the SWH in their classrooms, they may choose to begin small and target the generation of questions at the lesson level. In this case, student questions may be focused by observing a teacher demonstration, by having students observe demonstration stations, or by students putting their hands on simple equipment. The questions generated will be more targeted to the ideas in the lesson and the available equipment.

After the small groups have generated their questions, use some manner of classroom display such as sticky notes, butcher paper, or whiteboards. When displaying the questions, ask the class to evaluate the questions to help increase knowledge on the topic. A classification may also be used to rank the questions. Is the question essential, a "need to know" question, or a "nice to know" question? This strategy may be used to begin the SWH at the unit or lesson level or as a follow-up to the creation of concept maps. As part of the SWH approach, individual students may also generate questions for further study.

# Challenges

What challenges can you expect? Sometimes students are unwilling to generate any questions and this will require continuous reinforcement from you that the rules have changed and to be part of the class they will need to generate questions. The unwillingness may manifest itself through the development of ridiculous questions that have no connection to the unit but are designed to test your commitment to student control of their learning. This is a chance to practice classroom management, but don't get trapped into falling back into your old teaching strategies. If you can be manipulated by these questions to intervene and change the questions unilaterally, the SWH process won't flourish. Again, don't confuse classroom management with teaching and learning. You need to manage the classroom but also set the pace for learning. If in your professional judgment—as the one who must make the decisions for classroom control—a student is blocking the class from learning, by all means intervene. Do so in a way that moves the class toward learning. Don't react in a manner that moves the classroom to being controlled. Always move the classroom toward encouraging learning. Teaching needs to be in the service of learning.

Not every question that comes from the students will be a worthy question to investigate or research, but every question that comes from students will be their question. Helping students to generate questions that will further their understanding is a process, and it will take training in what is a good question.

Remember that the first step is getting students to ask questions; then we can help them refine their questions to make them better for inquiry and investigation. But what is a good question? The nature of scientifically oriented questions lends itself to empirical investigations that leads to gathering and using data to develop explanations of scientific phenomena. This type of question generates a "need to know." The answers to scientifically oriented questions can be based on observations and scientific knowledge obtained from reliable sources. In other words, they are either testable or researchable.

Also don't be afraid to put questions out in the discussion. As an equal in the discussion of ideas use a process of analysis to guide the question development. Use language such as, "I see that you have these similar questions. Can we group these and generate one question such as . . . ?" You can also provide questions but work to connect your question to the students' ideas so they can see the connection and feel ownership in the questions.

Testable questions may be characterized by the following characteristics:

❖ Begin with the word *what* or *how*

❖ Identify variables to control, manipulate, and measure

❖ Lead to experimentation

Researchable questions may be characterized by the following characteristics:

❖ Begin with *what*, *how*, or *why*

❖ Refer to relationships

❖ Lead to study from a variety of text-based and/or expert resources

Frequently, students generate *why* questions that probe origins. This type of question can often be refined into a *how* or *what* question that not only focuses student inquiries but also provides for more open-ended investigations. Our focus will be on testable questions.

In the following scenario, the teacher entered the SWH process by having students observe a teacher demonstration as a springboard to generate questions and then refine them using the characteristics of testable questions. The learning goal is around the idea of conservation of momentum.

## Scenario

Students observe two-wheeled carts on a track. One is stationary (Cart A) and the other (Cart B) is moving on the track toward the other. When Cart B crashes into Cart A, they stick together and both move off in the direction Cart B was originally moving. However, together they are moving more slowly than Cart B was initially moving and faster than Cart A, given that Cart A had been standing still.

After watching the carts and making observations, students are asked to generate questions about what they observed, record them, and share them in small groups. Then they must choose a few that seem most interesting to them and write them on sentence strips, chart paper, or whiteboards. These could be some of their original questions:

❖ Why did Cart B stick to Cart A?

❖ What is the mass of Cart A?

❖ What is the mass of Cart B?

❖ How does the mass of Cart A compare to Cart B?

❖ How fast are the carts going?

❖ How fast are the carts going before and after the crash?

To help students refine their questions to make them more testable, the teacher asks students to compare their brainstormed list of questions to the characteristics of testable questions discussed earlier in the year.

The teacher might support the students by asking questions such as:

❖ Which of the questions seem most testable and why?

❖ Which of the questions could be answered with short, factual information?

❖ Which questions identify variables we could test?

❖ Which questions try to get at relationships between or among variables?

❖ Which of the questions could really help guide an investigation?

In using the criteria, responding to these additional teacher questions, and making suggestions for revisions, the students recognize that many of their questions lead to information that they need to know and identify critical variables—mass and speed—but in their current form they don't help guide their investigation.

As students revise their questions, they might suggest the following as they build toward questions that will guide their investigations:

❖ What is the relationship between the mass and speed of Cart A and Cart B?

❖ How do the masses of Carts A and B affect the speeds of Carts A and B?

❖ What happens if Cart B is moving?

❖ How do the masses of Carts A and B affect the speeds of Carts A and B after the crash?

❖ How do the masses and speeds of Carts A and B before the collision affect the masses and speeds of Carts A and B after the collision?

❖ What happens if the carts don't stick together?

With teacher questions—"When thinking about these questions, how might you be more clear about the variables you will hold constant and the variables you will change?" and "For the moment, let's concentrate on what happens when the carts stick together. Can you live with that, knowing that we can test other scenarios next?"—students could further refine their questions with the following results:

1. What is the relationship between the masses and speeds of Carts A and B before the collision and the mass and speed of Cart A/B after the collision?

2. Holding the masses of Carts A and B and speed of Cart B constant, how does changing the speed of Cart A before the collision affect the speed of Cart A/B after the collision?

**3.** With constant speeds of Carts A and B, how does changing the mass of Cart A affect the speed of Cart A/B after the collision?

**4.** With constant speeds of Carts A and B, how does changing the mass of Cart B affect the speed of Cart A/B after the collision?

Students could use any of these questions to guide their investigation; however, questions 2, 3, and 4 will likely lead to an investigation yielding data that will reveal a pattern that leads to a claim that can be justified with evidence.

You have to decide how far to push students toward developing testable questions. If students become disengaged in the revisions, then the questions have lost their "punch" in that students will have lost ownership. Questions can be revised during the investigation. Remember, they are the students' questions—you know the big idea you are working toward and you can help guide students throughout the process.

In essence, good questions lead to learning. Testable questions lead to better investigations, which yield better evidence to use in justifying claims. Each step in this process requires students to think like a scientist and communicate their ideas.

## Teacher's Voice

When looking at getting students to ask good questions it can be more effective in talking about what didn't work. My students hit the whole spectrum and we started out with a free approach of letting students choose their own questions. The questions were all over the map. Most of them were meaningless and trivial questions. A lot of them were just yes/no questions. "Is this made of cells? Yes, I'm done." They saw no problem with that. That was ineffective, so I tried supplying the questions. And then they lost their investment in the meaning of it. The answer lies somewhere out there in the middle. And that's the trouble that we ran up against. I tried to make it a simpler process for what the students would work on in the lab. I thought this would make it easier for them to connect. It didn't. Then I tried letting them be all over the map and then find out the ineffectiveness of poor questions while working through the SWH. As the students worked they would try to get to focus on a new question that would be effective. That might have of been the most successful approach we had. They would try the question and say, "Oh, we can't figure this out. We can't do this. This is going nowhere." This would force them to go back and reconfigure their question based on what they learned working with their first question. There were also groups that would negotiate to come up with their own questions as a group. They would bring their own questions to the small lab groups and fight it out to get a quality question. This process was time intensive. I thought maybe a few, high-quality SWHs per year done in this way would be about all that they could handle. One SWH we tried took two or two-and-a-half weeks to really get through it. And that was just for one concept. It was worth it. They got it. I was hooked!

The first step is helping students generate good questions that look for relationships and identify variables using whatever language is appropriate for your school (for example, controlled vs. varied or independent vs. dependent). This is not to imply that all students have to have the perfect questions before they move on to investigate their questions. Having students work together to generate a few good questions to investigate early in the year and progressing to more independent question development is one way to help students build their skills. The key is having large- and small-group discussions to refine the questions they generate using the characteristics of testable questions.

You can guide students toward improved questions directly. When a student asks a question that is less than stellar, you can ask him or her to explain the value of the question with questions such as:

❖ How do you think this question will help you build your knowledge on the topic?

❖ Do you think that is a good question?

❖ How does your question compare to the criteria for a testable question?

The second strategy is to prompt classmates to take the lead in this process and ask the same kind of questions that you may want to ask. Try prompting another student to ask questions by having a quiet sidebar conversation. Ask the student what they think of the question and then prompt the student to ask the classmate about his or her concerns.

Another possible strategy would be to give the students a range of questions that you have generated and have them evaluate the questions based on criteria for a good question. This can be done either before or after they have done an SWH. If the class is typical they won't hold back in critiquing the teacher's questions. Then just turn their own standards back on their own work and ask them to follow their own standard. Students can also use these refined questions as models for generating future questions.

We know that students' first attempts will likely yield poor questions. As the teacher, you will need to control your impulse to step in, take over, and change questions. This can be a major step backward in your attempt to move toward a learner-centered classroom. Remember, the learner must take ownership of and accept the responsibility for his or her learning. With that line of thinking, no matter what the question, it is the student's question. If you overtly change questions, the message to the students will be that nothing has changed and they will fall back into the same old game.

This is not to say that your input in the question process is not critical—it is. You help shape the process and construct the learning environment. As the teacher, you will need to be clear about the unit learning goals identified during the planning process and have a pretty good sense of where students are with their prior knowledge. The recognition of the difference between where students are with their current understanding and where you want them to be will provide the basis for the questions or prompts you use with students. Before you even begin you will need to have anticipated where students' questions may go and be ready to help them move toward the unit learning goals. In many ways, you become a participant in the process—a fellow questioner—and at the same time you are required to be on top of where the class is and where you need them to go and be thinking of each next step.

The process of transitioning from a more traditional classroom to using the SWH may seem a little messy. The casual observer may not understand and may even think that when you "appear" to be a fellow questioner that you are "just sitting back and watching." He or she may even think that you are not doing your job. Nothing could be further from the truth. You are planning to help students achieve the unit learning goals, you are constantly assessing student progress, and you are constantly paying attention to the learning environment—this is exactly your job.

Be an advocate for your work with the SWH. Talk with your principal or department chair about what you are trying to do in your classroom. Work with your colleagues to get ideas and share challenges and successes. Talk with students and parents about your goals. Try to avoid the problem of the "casual observer." If someone walks into the classroom, invite him or her into the process. If you are stuck, say so and summarize for the visitor where you are in the process, or better yet, ask a student to summarize. If things are rolling along, the visitor will feel the energy and become just as engaged as the students! It may also be appropriate to engage the visitor in the process by asking what he or she thinks. Think how refreshing it might be for students to see a visiting adult struggle with the same ideas they are and in return, the visitor will have a better understanding of the hard work that you and your students are doing.

To help things "roll along," students need an attitude for learning. It may be necessary to invest some up-front class time to build a trust relationship where students build confidence in your commitment to this "new" way of learning.

Use strategies to help build students' questioning skills. One possibility is to use criteria for helping students generate good questions. Another is to provide students with question starters or examples of good questions. Consider letting students pursue "bad" questions and coming to dead ends or less than satisfying results. A positive classroom moment occurs when students find their question is not a good question, as in the following interchange:

STUDENT: This isn't working. Can I change my question?

TEACHER: Whose question is it?

STUDENT: Well, it's mine.

TEACHER: If it's your question, why are you asking me if you can change it?

In the questions step of the SWH, make sure you model your interest in the questions for what they can bring to the class and student learning. Be willing to learn right along with them by recognizing and saying that you can learn just as much as the students. This is about questions, not answers. Bite your tongue when you have the urge to give answers.

Some students' questions may be testable or researchable. Consider this question: What products will be generated by an accelerated proton striking a metal plate in a linear accelerator? This is a researchable question that can be tested but may not be of value in a high school classroom or possible within the limitations of most classrooms, given that most classrooms don't have a linear accelerator or access to one. This can be a tricky point. Very creative students may find ways to test questions that you have never considered. Remember that the question belongs to the student; get the student to consider whether he or she can test the question. Students may surprise you with some very creative and novel ways to get at knowledge. Desire to know can be a great motivator that pushes students to reach beyond what they would have typically been willing to do in your classroom.

The cliché that "a good question is one that leads to more questions" is true in the SWH approach. To achieve this goal a question must be open-ended—meaning that they can't be answered with a simple yes or no. To support students' refinement of their questions as well as work through subsequent stages in the SWH, the classroom environment needs to be characterized by trust and respect to support risk taking in sharing ideas and demonstrating skepticism.

The ground rules need to include management issues related to the students feeling safe to make their thinking public. If students are going to face derision and abuse for speaking out, you know that they won't be willing to share their thoughts with the class. Students also need to know that anytime they share their ideas, they need to be prepared to discuss them. Get everyone to accept the idea that they can't get away with "I don't know" as an easy way out. The students need to know that "I don't know" will be followed by more questions to get at what they do know. Thinking is required!

A key to creating this kind of classroom environment is to develop ground rules for public negotiation of ideas in a way that brings students into the process, so that they agree to work by these ground rules. You may find that students will invest a great deal more energy and thought into their discourse when it is being evaluated, challenged, shaped, or supported by their peers rather than by you, or in addition to you as teacher.

If the class agrees upon a standard for a good question, they should be able to measure the question against the standard. Remember, though, that a student could be so invested in his or her question that, no matter what the critique, he or she won't give an inch on that question.

As students progress they will begin to recognize that their questions aren't "good" questions. They will often ask, "Can I change my question?" As the teacher, consider whose questions these really are. If the students control their learning they can change their questions. As they become acclimated to the SWH approach these questions should disappear as they understand that the rules have changed and they can make their learning decisions openly.

The questions on page 109 vary in quality when viewed from the SWH perspective. The quality of the questions that students generated improved with each attempt at the SWH, which demonstrates improvement on the part of both teacher and students. Generating questions for the SWH is not a "one size fits all" endeavor, and various strategies work with different degrees of success with different students, different content, and different teachers. This is something that requires practice and patience.

Once questions are selected, the SWH will flow into the next stage in which students test their question(s). Remember, the better the question, the more focused the investigation, and the more likely that students will be able to make a claim and support it with evidence collected during their investigation.

This section provides a framework to help you think about how to help students generate testable questions. The vignettes and scenarios offer concrete examples of the ways in which various teachers and their students have struggled and succeeded in their efforts.

In the next section, we'll consider the following questions:

❖ How will students design investigations around their questions?

❖ How will students conduct their investigations and collect data based on their questions?

❖ How can we maintain a focus on student learning?

❖ How can we establish and maintain a safe learning environment?

❖ How will students organize data?

❖ How can students represent data to reveal patterns and relationships?

We'll provide ideas about what students need to be able to do to be successful as well as practical suggestions for helping students build these skills.

## From the Students

Samples of student questions: A list of student questions that come from classrooms of teachers that have begun using the SWH follows. These sample questions are from early attempts at the SWH and show the improvement.

*Tenth-grade Biology*

Genetics Unit SWH 1

❖ Where do traits, such as red hair, come from? Can you still pure breed today?

❖ Where do genetic diseases come from?

❖ What was this lab suppose to show (teach) us?

❖ What is the law of segregation?

Genetics Unit SWH 2

❖ How can one ear of corn have two different-colored kernels, and come up with a ratio? Which color is more dominant? What are the parent's genotypes and phenotypes?

❖ Are black and white dominant? Which color of kernel is more popular?

❖ Why does one ear have more black than white?

❖ What color is dominant?

❖ What are the possible genotypes for the corn parents? How many different phenotypes can occur and what are they? What color is dominant for the kernels?

*Seventh-grade Life Science*

Cell SWH 1

❖ Do fruits and vegetables have cells?

❖ Did cells grow inside?

❖ Can I find cells in fruits and vegetables?

Cell SWH 2

❖ What effect does salt water have on elodea?

❖ What effect does regular water have on elodea?

❖ How do different fluids affect the elodea cells?

# How Will Students Design Investigations Around Their Questions?

With a good question in hand, students begin to think about the kind of information that they may need to collect. This constitutes the second phase of the SWH—*Tests: What did I do?* Just as scientists would do, students may need opportunities to try out their ideas before they commit to a procedure for collecting data and a way to organize their data. Students will also need different levels of support to help them think about how to design their investigation. For some questions or content, they may need lots of guidance in designing an investigation, whereas for others they may be able to work more independently.

For example, the first time students use a new piece of equipment such as a compound microscope or computer probeware, they will need support in designing an experiment. Students may need to use trial and error or another problem-solving strategy to perfect their data collection methods in some cases, while in others, you may choose to provide more guidance to allow students to focus on more critical issues or to save time. Students may also need more support when using a new technique such as pipetting.

Different levels of student experience will also affect the decision regarding the amount of support they will need to design their investigation. On one end of the spectrum, some students have lots of questions and great ideas for investigations but lack the ability to get their ideas down on paper in any kind of organized way. On the other end of the spectrum, some students are meticulous and organized but may struggle to generate ideas. If students don't seem to have either gift, then there's certainly room for growth!

In a classroom, we can expect students with a wide variety of experiences. The challenge is to provide opportunities for all students to recognize and appreciate their own abilities as well as the abilities of others and then take the next step in identifying areas for improvement and making progress in those areas—all while learning about the big ideas of science. It seems like a daunting task, but the SWH can help!

In the earlier section on questioning, we talked about how teachers bring their knowledge and skills to bear to help guide students in developing questions. The same knowledge and skills will be necessary to guide students in taking the next steps in the process. To help students improve their skills in designing investigations, you may want to provide a series of guiding questions. These might include:

❖ What variables are identified in your question?

❖ What materials and equipment will you need?

❖ What regular increment will you use for your independent variable? (For example, if you are controlling for time, what time increment will be needed?) If you don't know what the increment should be, how could you find out?

❖ What conditions will need to be kept the same? How will you make sure that you are keeping those conditions the same?

❖ How will you communicate your procedure? (For example, you have to write it down and draw a picture of your equipment setup.)

❖ What safety precautions will you need to observe?

❖ As you are collecting data, how will you know that your data makes sense?

❖ How will you organize your data (for example, construct a data table, record qualitative observations)?

The language in these questions may need to be changed to match the language from your standards or assessments.

It takes a lot of time to design an investigation. Sometimes students might use standard procedures that they modify for their specific question (for example, steps to change the pH of a solution). Another option is to generate a class question and design an investigation where each group is collecting data that will be compiled for everyone to use (for example, the affect of various temperature changes on daphnia). A third option is to provide students with the procedure but have them create the data table. The key is for students to have many experiences throughout the year and throughout their school career of designing investigations around their questions. This all needs to be held in tension with the students' level of sophistication and knowledge to design appropriate tests in addition to available materials.

## Teacher's Voice

In my junior-senior-level physics classroom, we use computer probeware including photogates, motion detectors, smart pulleys, and force probes to help us collect data and look for patterns as we study Newton's Laws of Motion. My standard practice is to provide each group of students with a set of probes and tell them where the software for each probe is located in the folder system. I also go through the file-naming protocol to use when each lab group saves their trials. (I always keep a clean version of the software in a protected folder in case of a "saving" error.) Using the instructions that come with the probes, each lab group connects their probes and tests them. I also help them learn to adjust time intervals so that they can design their own experiments.

As often as possible, I bring physics students in to help my physical science students learn to use the probeware—I only introduce one probe at a time with younger students. With a junior or senior working with two or three lab groups, I know that my older students establish an appropriate level of fun and model an appropriate level of care for the equipment.

As you think about the overall process and questions described earlier, keep in mind that the design of the investigation is part of the SWH. This is not a time to go back and use a verification lab activity. However, text resources may be useful to you as you set up demonstration stations to help students generate questions or as students learn to use equipment or specialized techniques.

As students are working in small groups to design their investigations, it's important that the teacher move about the room and ask students open-ended questions to help prompt their thinking and guide their work. These might include the questions used to help them design their investigations (described previously) or other questions or prompts such as:

- ❖ Where are you in your design process?
- ❖ What are you struggling with most?
- ❖ How does this part of your design connect to your question?
- ❖ What parts of your design do you think are strongest? Weakest?
- ❖ I noticed that Jen's lab group was struggling with the same issue. Why don't you send a scout over to listen to their ideas?
- ❖ How many trials do you think you'll need to conduct to be sure you have reliable data?

Other questions might begin with phrases such as:

- ❖ What might you do to . . . ?
- ❖ How could you . . . ?
- ❖ What do you think will happen when you or if you . . . ?

Other ideas were presented in Chapter 3 including how important it is for teachers to provide opportunities for students to work "through what data to collect and how best to represent this data." This means avoiding the temptation to provide an empty data table. It's critical that students "wrestle with trying to understand what the activity is asking of them," rather than the teacher "telling them what to do and when." Emphasis is also placed on the benefits of having students or student groups collect different data so that "when the whole class is discussing the results they are required to think more broadly." This will require students to account for both patterns and variations in the data. Rather than having the activity confirm what the teacher said or vice versa, students will use the data to justify their ideas.

# How Will Students Conduct Their Investigations and Collect Data Around Their Questions?

Throughout the SWH approach, the teacher has to pay attention to student learning and classroom management. During this phase of the SWH where students are testing their ideas, classroom management can be the most challenging due to safety concerns. The bottom line is how can we provide an appropriate balance between a free-for-all and a teacher-controlled classroom? How does the teacher provide a safe environment where students can conduct their investigations and learn by doing science?

# How Can We Maintain a Safe Learning Environment?

To maintain a safe learning environment, you may want to start by making a list of the management strategies that you currently use and then consider how they affect student learning and then generate some ideas about how you will help students stay focused on the inquiry. You will also want to consider strategies to help manage materials in a way that keeps them ready to use for the next class.

As teachers, we need to set clear expectations for behavior and follow through with consequences. When students are engaged with their own questions, most will stay focused and do their work. A few will test the limits. Be prepared for those tests and nip behavior problems in the bud, right from the very first experience.

## Teacher's Voice

Working with students with all their own questions was a challenge at first. I had to move constantly asking questions, watching, and listening. I found that many students saw switching to this classroom was an open invitation to test the new ground rules. Management of the classroom was just as important as ever, and I needed to have a sense of what was going on with each group of students. When students were off-task or didn't want to play by the new rules I simply gave them a choice. They could get back on task or they could go back to the "old way" of doing things and do standard classroom activities. This wasn't a punishment, just a choice that let students choose how they would learn. It was all about giving students control of their learning, not the classroom.

Classroom management will be most effective when you show genuine interest in what they are learning and what they are doing to learn. This means asking questions about their work rather than asking questions to monitor their work. The question, "What are you doing?" sounds very different when asked for these two purposes.

Materials management provides another challenge. Some classroom teachers use a "tub" approach. Each lab group has a tub of equipment that they take to their workspace, use, and return to the storage space. In this case, the teacher checks the tub before the end of the class period to see that all the contents are present, clean, and organized. If not, the group is asked to correct the problem. For others, setting equipment and materials out where students can gather what they need is successful when students take responsibility for returning materials and equipment to the table in the condition in which they were found—or better. Other teachers may use the rotating role of "materials manager" for each working group of students. The key is to set up routines for the "things" that support learning, so that you can spend time *and* energy talking with students about their learning.

If classroom management is a concern, find someone in your building who has a knack for it and visit his or her classroom and/or talk with him or her about the strategies used. You might also consider videotaping your classroom or the classroom of others as a way to improve classroom management skills—or for that matter, focus on the kinds of questions or prompts used to advance student learning. The bottom line is that good classroom management provides an environment for learning knowing that the only person who controls the learning is the student.

One of the benefits of using the SWH is the constant focus on learning as students are engaged in learning around their own questions. With thoughtful interventions, management takes care of itself.

## How Can We Maintain a Focus on Student Learning?

One way to maintain a focus on student learning is to continually reinforce the student as learner, not the teacher as "explainer." Teacher questioning strategies are important throughout all phases of the SWH and will be especially critical here as students really begin to wrestle with science concepts as they design and conduct their investigations.

While you are moving around the room—let me say that again because your constant attention and proximity is critical—while you are moving around the room, your questioning skills will be put to the test. Students will ask for answers. You have to respond with more questions. One indication of the success of the SWH is when students stop seeing you as the answer-giver. Another is when students precede their questions with what they know, what they think they know, and then follow with the question about what they think they need to know or where they are stuck. The real challenge in knowing what question to ask of a student or group of students is based in three ideas:

❖ What do students already know about the topic? (What is their prior knowledge?)

❖ What big idea of science is the focus for this inquiry? (What do we want students to learn?)

❖ What do they need to consider to promote their learning? (How can we help them close the gap between what they already know and an understanding of the big idea of science?)

When students ask a question, try to respond with, "What do you think?" as a way of turning back the question. Other questions might include, "How could you find that out?" or "What do you think would happen if you tried that?" or "Why is that important?"

Another challenge is to know when and how far to push students. When students show a level of frustration that concerns you, try reminding them to breathe or, if appropriate, get them to laugh to relieve the stress. Then you can try another tack. Perhaps you could ask them to think about something they did earlier in the year or the unit that might help them make a connection. You might also ask them to think about another student's comment. Try paraphrasing their concerns so that they know that you recognize their frustration and understand their question. If the paraphrase doesn't capture their current thinking, they'll tell you and you can try again. Enlist their team members to help. Create the sense that we are all in this together! An indication of the success of teacher questioning strategies is how well students begin to ask questions of themselves and of others. Encourage students to ask questions of one another as they conduct their investigations. They can learn from their team members and other groups about what works and what doesn't.

Sometimes students will look to you for the easy answers when they really need to struggle and think for themselves. For this situation, you may want to select a personal mantra that you recite when they ask you a question. For example, you could respond by saying something like, "I have never seen that before. What do you think?" If you are diligent and consistent you will get students to be independent. Isn't that a major goal, to develop lifelong learners?

In the course of the conversation with students, it may become apparent that they do need additional information. As indicated earlier, one source of information is other students. Other sources of information would include text resources (such as books, journals, or the Internet) or experts (for example, scientists or teachers). You are the most ready source of information and you will find times when you do provide students with needed information. The key is achieving an appropriate balance as you maintain a focus on student learning and constantly reinforce the idea that the student has the responsibility for and ownership of his or her own learning.

Consider yourself a physician who is treating a patient. You need to constantly diagnose where the patient is and what needs to be done next. And on top of that you need to get the patient to move toward the correct treatment without being able to tell him or her what to do. You can only direct the patient by helping him or her identify what he or she needs to do by questioning. You will find yourself exhausted at the end of the day when you shift teaching this way.

## Teacher's Voice

Moving to student-centered learning required constant evaluation of learning experiences; this was a difficult skill to develop and it took practice. I found myself in the middle of a lesson and became disoriented and fell back into my traditional style of teaching. Even though I didn't give up I often wanted to. But I reassess where we are and tell the class what is happening. I am open and model the process for them. I think of the process of one of dialogue between every person in the room, literally. When anyone steps into the classroom he or she has to engage in the process so I negotiate my understanding of my teaching publicly with students. It was scary at first but it turned out to be a great thing. We all became colleagues on a personal course of learning. We cultivated a culture of dialogue based on negotiating meaning from the dialogue. Students loved it when the principal came into the room and had to join with the students who would engage him in the same process of give and take of ideas. Every time someone visits our class and discussion about ideas is occurring I would ask the visitor what he or she thinks about what is being said and then get students to follow up with questions to challenge or clarify. Students find this empowering, and it gives vivid reinforcement to the atmosphere you are trying to create, an atmosphere of "all must think and defend thoughts."

## How Will Students Organize Their Data?

As students design and conduct their investigation, they also need to consider how they will organize the data that they collect. This is the third phase of the SWH: *Observations: What did I find?* Helping students learn to create data tables and then record their data is an important step in the process. Students may also need to consider the kinds of observations that will need to be made. Seeing a well-organized data table is one indication that students have considered the relevant variables.

A possible strategy for helping students learn to create data tables is to provide models of various data tables and then have students create their own tables based on the models. Examples of data representation tables are displayed in Figure 6.3, 6.4, and 6.5.

Another option would be to use a thinkaloud strategy to talk through how you, as the teacher, would go about creating a data table. Students could also be asked to use this strategy as they share with the class the data tables they've created.

As students try out some of their ideas, they will need to record their findings. This seems like such a simple thing, but again, it can be a challenge. Initially, you'll need to spend time and energy reminding students to get their ideas down on paper. You might consider using notebook strategies so that students keep all of their information in one place and can reflect back on their progress over the course of several SWH experiences.

Different groups of students may be collecting data that needs to be compiled to reveal patterns. This kind of accountability can be motivating and can also save time. For example, each group may be testing the effect of a different set of temperatures or pH on solubility or daphnia behavior. This data will need to be pulled together in a class data table for analysis. (It might be worth noting here that these are activities you might have done as a traditional verification lab. The difference here is the process used to enter the lab—using student questions and student-designed investigations.)

Students will also need to learn to represent their data in a variety of ways to better communicate their findings, including the use of graphs or diagrams. In more traditional approaches, students may use these skills in an isolated activity. The SWH provides an opportunity for students to represent their own data in a way that helps them make and support their claim.

# How Can Students Represent Data to Reveal Patterns and Relationships?

Students must consider how their data might be represented to reveal patterns or relationships. For example, does the data lend itself to graphing, and if so, what kind of graph is most appropriate? As they consider the nature of the graph, they'll also need to use basic graphing skills to determine the variables that belong on the X- and

## From the Students

**Figure 6.3.** *Date representations example*

For example:

| Total Time | Total Distance | Trial Observations |
|---|---|---|
|  |  |  |
|  |  |  |

| Time Interval | pH | *Daphnia* Observations |
|---|---|---|
|  |  |  |
|  |  |  |

| Height | Speed | Trial Observations |
|---|---|---|
|  |  |  |
|  |  |  |

| Type of Fluid | *Elodea* Observations |
|---|---|
|  |  |
|  |  |

*continues on next page*

**Figure 6.4.** *Acid/base data table from an SWH student*

II. Observations

How does solid chemicals: Iron mg zn.cu. change pH of acids and bases?

| | Initial | Iron | Mg | Zinc | Cu |
|---|---|---|---|---|---|
| NaOH 6M | pH ~ 11 | 11 | 11 | 11 | 11 |
| HC₂H₃O₂ 6M | pH ~ 3 | 3 | Mg dissolved sizzled 5 | little bubble 3 | 3 |
| HCl 6M | pH ~ 1 | bubbles. turned 2 yellowish green. Fe didn't dissolve | more reaction than HC₂H₃O₂ 1 Mg dissolved faster | sizzled. bad smell 1 more reaction than HC₂H₃O₂ | 1 |
| NaOH 1M | pH ~ 11 | 11 | 11 | 11 | 11 |

\* Bases don't react with solids

**Figure 6.5.** *Ramps data table*

Magnus 4/4   9/13   √S2

| Test Trial # | Distance (cm) | Force (N) Fast | Force (N) Slow | Time (sec.) Fast | Time (sec.) Slow |
|---|---|---|---|---|---|
| 1 | 110 cm | .5N | .8N | 4.28 sec round 4 sec | 16.65 sec 17 sec |
| Long 2 | 110 cm | .6N | .6N | 4.63 sec round 4 sec | 12.88 sec 13 sec |
| 3 | 110 cm | .5N | .6N | 3.13 sec round 3 sec | 14.5 sec 15 sec |
| Avg by trials add everything | 110 cm | .53N | .66N | 3.813 sec round 4 sec | 14.476 14 sec |
| 1 | 110 cm | .7N | .7N | 6.47 sec round 6 sec | 11.07 sec 11 sec |
| Short 2 | 110 cm | .6 N | .7N | 5.80 sec round 6 sec | 14.33 sec 14 sec |
| 3 | 110 cm | .9N | .7N | 3.14 sec round 3 sec | 14.5 sec 14 sec |
| Avg. | 110 cm | .73N | .7N | 4.98 sec round 5 sec | 13.23 sec 13 sec |

④

Y-axes as well as determine the most appropriate scale for each axis. Students will also need to use proper labeling techniques so that the reader can make sense of the graph.

Students will need support in using computer or graphing calculator applications to generate graphs and produce best-fit lines as they consider what the slopes of trend lines might represent. It's also possible that students will know more about these technologies than we as teachers do—take advantage of this resource. If you're having trouble with the graphing calculators, downloading the software, or calibrating the probes, let students help! It can save you time and energy and provide students with those specific skills an opportunity to excel.

Students may need to learn to support their observations with diagrams or draw models of their ideas. Clear rubrics, scoring guidelines, and/or examples of student work can be very helpful in communicating your expectations clearly. Pull examples of student work from your most current learning activity and make copies for posting the next time you do this activity. You might choose examples of high-, medium-, and low-quality work and make comments on the work about what the student has done and what would make the work better. These work samples and comments serve as a model that students can use to self-assess the quality of their diagrams or models.

In this phase of the SWH, students work together to generate and bounce ideas off one another as they create graphs or models and analyze their data. Lab activities often are designed with the data collection structure already determined. As students work with more data they need the room to experiment on how they represent the data from their tests. Encourage students to begin with the data in mind as they begin to design their tests. Don't prescribe the data system. Instead promote various versions and ask questions about the way data will be represented. Ask questions that will push students to consider the options for looking at the data and promote student-to-student talk around the data representation. Tables, graphs, photographs, descriptions, and other methods may be appropriate methods and how each young scientist represents the data allows the students to explore different ways to look for patterns and relationships in the data. By encouraging multiple data forms class discussions about the relative merits of each system will push them to deeper understanding of understanding data, which can be a very sophisticated process.

As the SWH process unfolds it's important to help students make connections among the question(s) they ask, the investigation they design, the data they collect and organize, how they make a claim based on the information collected, and how to support the claim with evidence. Just as students need lots of experience designing and conducting investigations, they also need lots of experience analyzing data to make a claim and construct an argument to support their claim using evidence from their investigations. Students often begin to struggle with forming a claim based on their tests' evidence and discover that the data has no connection to the question and can't be formed into a claim. At this point they can become frustrated, but with support they can go back to the question and examine it in light of their experience and then reshape the question based on their new experience and understanding.

In the next sections, we'll consider the following questions:

❖ How will students use the evidence collected in their investigations to make a claim?

❖ How will students support their claim using the evidence collected during their investigation?

# How Will Students Use Their Data to Make a Claim?

Through the SWH, students write a statement that answers their question as part of the fourth phase of the SWH: *Claims: What inferences can I make?* This statement is their claim. When thinking about the process of connecting claims and evidence, it may seem like the question, "Which came first, the chicken or the egg?" When students analyze and evaluate their data by looking for relationships and patterns, they begin to develop a claim that in turn can be supported by the patterns or relationships that emerge from their data.

Without being too algorithmic, a structure for writing a claim can be helpful as students develop their skills. For example, guide students with a simple statement such as:

My question was _____. I think _____.

The following samples provide a range of examples of SWH work by students on various topics and for various grade ranges. As you look at these samples compare the questions to the claims and evidence.

# How Do We Get Students to Understand What Is Evidence and What Is Opinion?

Separating data from opinion and then assembling that into the basis for building an argument that explains a question is a difficult and challenging process. Several possible and popular methods can help students begin to understand the relationship between these different forms of information. All too often students equate data,

# From the Students

**Figure 6.6.** *Student SWH samples: These samples show a range of skill in forming questions and then generating claims and evidence*

Science Writing Heuristic Template

121/21

Name_____

Hour G

Date 12-1

Science Writing Heuristic Lab:_____

| 1. Beginning ideas...What questions do I have? |
|---|
| What colors are the ink |

| 2. Tests...What did I do? (How did you test to answer your questions?) |
|---|
| 1.pour water into the container<br>2.draw a line 3cm from bottom<br>3.Plot X every cm.<br>4.put the S inks on Xs<br>5 Let ink dry<br>6 tip ink in for 15 mins. |

3. Observations...What did I find? (What did you find when you tested?)

**Figure 6.6.** *(Continued)*

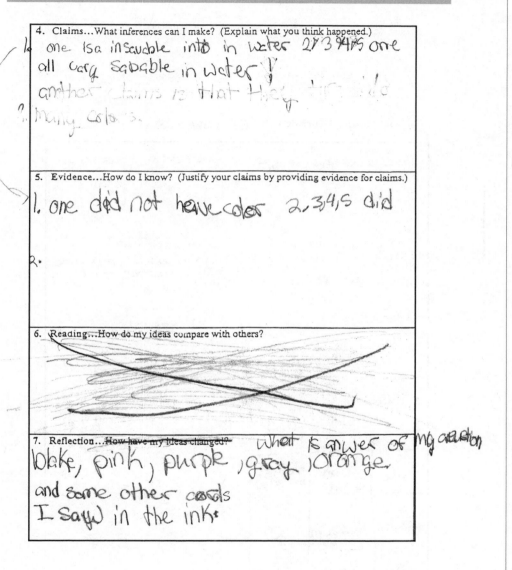

4. Claims...What inferences can I make? (Explain what you think happened.)

1. one Isa insauble into in water 2,3 4,5 one all cary sabable in water.
another claims is that they tir ido
2. many colors.

5. Evidence...How do I know? (Justify your claims by providing evidence for claims.)

1. one did not have color 2,3,4,5 did

2.

6. Reading...How do my ideas compare with others?

7. Reflection...How have my ideas changed?     What is anwer of my question

blake, pink, purple, gray, orange
and some other cools
I saw in the ink.

*continues on next page*

**Figure 6.6.** *(Continued)*

Science Writing Heuristic Template

Name _____
Hour _3̶ᵃ̶_
Date _11-13_

Science Writing Heuristic Lab: Pendulum Lab

1. Beginning ideas...What questions do I have?

How will the length of the string effect how many swings per sec.

2. Tests...What did I do? (How did you test to answer your questions?)

Tested a pendulum at 100cm & 50cm and timed them for 30 sec. each. The shorter the string the faster the swing.

3. Observations...What did I find? (What did you find when you tested?")

| Time | String Length | Swings in 30s. |
|------|---------------|----------------|
| 30s. | 100cm | 30 |
| 30. | 50cm | 39 |

**Figure 6.6.**   *(Continued)*

4.  **Claims**…What inferences can I make?  (Explain what you think happened.)

The longer the string the slower the swings, and the shorter the string the faster the swings are.

5.  **Evidence**…How do I know?  (Justify your claims by providing evidence for claims.)

Longer String (100cm) for 30sec = 30 swings
Shorter String (50cm) for 30 sec = 39 swings

6.  Reading…How do my ideas compare with others?

Kinetic energy - energy in the form of motion
Potential energy - stored energy

7.  **Reflection**…How have my ideas changed?

*continues on next page*

**Figure 6.6.** *(Continued)*

Science
Writing
Heuristic        20/21

Science Writing Heuristic Template

Name_____
Hour **4th**
Date **10/28**

Science Writing Heuristic Lab: "What is a solution"

---

1. Beginning ideas...What questions do I have?

Of these 6 cups which ones are Solutions?

---

2. Tests...What did I do? (How did you test to answer your questions?)

1. powder drink mix 3, water
2. rubbing alchol 3, water
3. MilK 3, water
4. Sugar/water           and...?
5. Oil/water
6. baking soda/salt

---

3. Observations...What did I find? (What did you find when you tested?)

| Observation | Tyndell |
|---|---|
| 1 <u>yes</u> solution only see one liquid | 1 yes |
| 2 <u>yes</u> you can only see one | 2 yes |
|  | 3 yes |
| 3 <u>no</u> the milk is heavyer and goes to the bottom | 4 No |
| 4 <u>yes</u> the sugar floats on top dissolved | 5 No |
| 5 the oil floats on the water <u>no</u> | 6 no |
| 6 <u>No</u> you can see both of the objects mixed. |  |

**Figure 6.6.**  *(Continued)*

**Claim overall**

4. Claims...What inferences can I make? (Explain what you think happened.)

1 yes dizolwed

2 yes dissolwed

3 no

4 no } won't dissolve and you can

5 no } see that their two.

6 no

5. Evidence...How do I know? (Justify your claims by providing evidence for claims.)

**Evidence**

1 you can only see one liquid & the powder dizzolved.

2 you can only see one liquid & the tyndell methad works to say yes

3 you can see that the milk is more towads the bottom it's split a 1/2 of the way down from the top.

4 the sugar floats on the top and makes weird bubbles but the suger dissolved in the liquid

5 the oil floates on the top

6 look carefuly you can see powder o softbaking soda and crystals as of salt

6. Reading...How do my ideas compare with others?

number four used to be a no not a yes the bubbles on the top confused me

7. Reflection...How have my ideas changed?

Solutions are always clear and the two materials have become one.

opinion, and evidence when in reality they are very different. Teachers have used a legal system model to help students understand the differences between the three. Based on the popularity of "CSI-like" television shows, the idea of courtroom argument can serve as a useful tool to get at the differences between data and opinion and can then help students understand how data becomes evidence. If students begin to approach their SWH investigations as legal arguments they can transfer the model they see in popular television shows and movies. At the end of the SWH the student/scientist/lawyer will need to convince a classroom of peers that his or her argument explaining the question is valid based on the evidence, which the student built from the data. To achieve a persuasive argument the student must interpret the data. Patterns that can be observed help tell a story from the data. The role of a scientist is to take data and see meaningful patterns in the data that aren't often obvious. As student-scientists data patterns often do not jump out at the students, and the way the data is represented either can be helpful or may get in the way. By comparing data across a class, students may be able to see patterns in other data representations other than their own, and by comparing data representations students can become better at building evidence as well as managing data.

Continuing with the courtroom model, as students begin to make claims about their questions the obvious question becomes, "What is your evidence? Where did you get that evidence?" This social argumentation sharpens the students' skills at interpreting data as well as clarifies their understanding of the "big ideas" of the unit.

To begin the development of these young scientist-lawyers, the following exercise helps clarify data and opinion and their application to a claim. "Mr. Xavier," developed by James Rudd, helps students use data to begin to form evidence that leads to a claim.

> **HAVE A GO!**
> **MAKING CLAIMS, PROVIDING EVIDENCE**
>
> Mr. Xavier is a mystery scenario designed to help students develop skills and understanding in claims and evidence. Go to Appendix K to engage in this exercise of developing claims and evidence.

## How Will Students Support Their Claim with Evidence?

In the fifth phase of the SWH: *Evidence: How do I know?*, students use the information gathered to justify their claim. In some types of investigation, *all* the data collected constitutes evidence. In other types of investigations and most research, only some of the data or information collected constitutes evidence. For the most part, we are not particularly good at differentiating between data and evidence, and if we aren't very good at it as teachers, it's hard to help students be clear about the relationship between the two ideas.

What is evidence? Often students will write, "See Data" as their evidence. This clearly indicates that the student does not understand the difference between data and evidence. Data is data. Evidence is the representation of the data in a form that undergirds an argument that works to answer the original question. We are constantly bombarded with evidence but often don't see it as such. Think of the scientific debates through the ages as well as those that are currently being argued. Evolution, global warming, health risks of smoking, eat butter, don't eat butter, and on and on. These arguments at some point look at the same data, and yet scientists come to widely differing claims. If you strip away all the politics and other motivations, how can two people come to such different conclusions based on the same data? Evidence is the answer. The story built from the data that leads to a claim is the evidence. Many teachers have used the analogy of a courtroom argument to help students understand the concept of evidence.

Consider human impact on the global climate as an example. Scientists have access to the same data. The differences that result in their conclusions results from what they do with the data, what data they choose to include or discard, and the patterns they see in the data. This can be confusing and often people look at science as unreliable because of the range of interpretations that can come from data. That really is the beauty of science: It is the public negotiation that seeks a common agreement based on claims and evidence that moves scientific understanding forward.

Evidence is the foundation of a claim and the negotiations that follow. The strongest negotiation comes from the most well-crafted argument that tells the best story in answering the question. The evidence should be a persuasive argument built from the data and observations. An explanation that makes the best attempt at answering the question based on the data observed in an understandable and thorough argument stands up best in the public negotiation for understanding, both in the classroom and the science community.

What precedes the evidence also affects the result. Generally, the better and more focused the question, the more likely students will collect data that constitutes evidence that leads to a claim. Tests that best get at the question produce data that is most effective in developing an answer. Consider the diagram in Figure 6.7, which represents the relationship between data and evidence.

Students may collect some data that will not contribute to making a claim because it doesn't directly relate to the question or doesn't yield a pattern. That portion of the data that both relates to the question (or produces new questions) and yields a pattern can be considered evidence. This is the information that contributes to a reasoned and logical justification of their claim. In some types of investigations (especially those

## From the Students

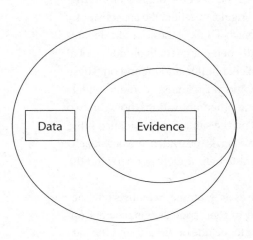

Students may collect some data that will not contribute to making a claim because it doesn't directly relate to the question or doesn't yield a pattern. That portion of the data that both relates to the question (or produces new questions) and yields a pattern can be considered evidence. This is the information that contributes to a reasoned and logical justification of their claim. In some types of investigations (especially those involving research), all the data may constitute evidence while in others only a portion will.

We must not forget the benefits of data that don't answer the proposed question but actually raise new questions. We also must not forget that science is often messy and that the unexpected result can be the most powerful.

---

involving research), all the data may constitute evidence while in others only a portion will constitute evidence.

We must not forget the benefits of data that don't answer the proposed question but actually raise new questions. We also must not forget that science is often messy and that the unexpected result can be the most powerful.

We must not forget the benefits of data that don't answer the proposed question but actually raise new questions. We must not forget that often science is messy and the unexpected result can be the most powerful.

Just as a good question can lead to the collection of data that is more likely to be considered evidence, good data organization can lead to more efficient and effective analysis that helps to uncover the patterns or relationships in the data that constitute evidence.

# How Can Students Use Evidence to Support Their Claim?

In the next phase of the process, the claim is supported by the evidence collected from the investigation in a way that provides a reasoned and logical account of the student's thinking. Students need to connect their ideas. Students might use sentences such as the following:

Since _____, then _____.
The pattern in the data revealed _____.
When _____, then _____.
The graph showed a _____ relationship between _____ and
_____.

Students will also need to be encouraged to use labeled diagrams or pictures to help support their claims. This provides another opportunity to post student work samples that students can use to assess their own work. Some of the work samples may be of low quality in which common errors might be highlighted. For example, one thing that we wouldn't want to see a student write is "see data table."

## Teacher's Voice

I have become more convinced that students must be given opportunities to build their own learning based on their own ideas and built on their own experiences, and to communicate to others with their own understanding; I have realized the power that this can bring to the classroom. But I would not be honest if I didn't also say that it has brought some dilemmas for me personally as well. One area in which I constantly struggle is monitoring the questioning and the discussion in class. I firmly believe that students must have opportunities to make decisions about what will be done and how it will be done, and these decisions need to be discussed and debated publicly. I also believe that in the process of negotiating, kids will build up and solidify their understanding of the topics they participate in and debate about. I am always concerned about how long I need to let the discussions go on if they appear to be veering in a direction away from the conceptual "big ideas" that we have set out to guide our learning. I also sometimes struggle with the fact that if I have thirty students in the classroom, and one student has a very passionate interest or belief about a particular topic, but it appears very few others do, is it my responsibility to shift the discussion away from this or is that inhibiting the passionate student's chances to learn? As I have become more aware of the power of students' questions and their own curiosity to drive learning in my classroom, I have also started to worry in some cases more about my actions cutting off valuable learning opportunities. It is difficult to find a balance between allowing all students to have their say and pursue their interests and their questions through investigations, and yet still trying to support everyone in a group of high school students to reach some scientifically supported consensus on a conceptual big idea in science. I am sure that at times student questions in my class go unanswered, but I am confident that that happens much less now, and that a greater percentage of them are answered, dealt with, and used to help us all form a better understanding of our scientific topics.

## Revisiting the Big Idea

Generating an argument is an important step in thinking and working like a scientist and in communicating scientific ideas. This argument involves justifying a claim with evidence and is at the heart of learning science. When the question and investigation are focused on a big idea of science, the construction of a claim and explanation will contribute to student understanding of the big ideas of science. In the next phase of the SWH approach, students will continue to think and work like scientists as they compare their ideas to those of others. The next chapter describes the last phase of the SWH process as students reflect not only on *what* they learned but also *how* they learned it.

# CHAPTER 7

# Reading and Reflection

Earlier in this text you read the following paragraph:

> Two quotes are important when we talk about learning. The first is by Strike (1987, p. 483) who stated "philosophically the suggestion that people are active in learning or knowledge construction is rather uninteresting. It is uninteresting because almost no one, beyond a few aberrant behaviorists, denies it." This quote sets the stage for our thinking over the last fifteen years and underpins the basis for all the curriculum reform documents brought out in the '90s. The National Science Education Standards (NRC, 1996) place great emphasis on the need for students to be active learners, to inquire and be curious about science, and to communicate their understandings to others. (This text, page 22)

The preceding chapters described how students use the SWH process to generate questions, design investigations to collect data, and construct claims supported by the evidence collected. Throughout the process so far, students have negotiated meaning for themselves as individuals and through conversation with others, or "dialogical interactions."

A logical question arises at this point and needs to be addressed. What do we do when students' claims are incomplete or inconsistent with current scientific thinking—in other words, they are wrong? What do we do when the data that students have collected and used to justify their claims is inaccurate? What do we do when students have not constructed a logical and reasoned argument using their evidence? In this chapter, we'll address these concerns and consider the role of the teacher in helping students connect their work to the body of knowledge that is science.

In a traditional classroom, students may have engaged in "verification labs." Students' claims and evidence may be put into a conclusion section of a lab report and this act ends the process. In the SWH approach, students' claims and evidence are really just the beginning as students continue negotiating meaning. The final two steps it the SWH approach are:

❖ *Reading: How do my ideas compare with others?*

❖ *Reflection: How have my ideas changed?*

Some of the richest negotiation for meaning can happen in the Reading and Reflection stages if you use strategies that help students make connections with existing science knowledge and challenge student thinking.

## Checking with the Experts: Reading to Gain New Understandings

The Reading stage is designed to have a dual purpose: 1) to continue to promote ownership and maintain the focus on the learner's control of his or her own learning, and 2) to promote ongoing negotiation of meaning as the learner considers the value of his or her ideas with others and in comparison to the ideas of others. At this point, students will have their own question with their own answer. Whether that answer is "right" or "wrong," students have an investment in their current understanding about the big ideas or concepts. As a teacher, you are well aware of reality—students will have a wide range of ideas at this point. That range presents a teaching dilemma. Should you as teacher correct the students' ideas and tell them the "right" answer or continue to defer to the learners' control of learning and stay the course—letting them sort it out themselves?

As mentioned earlier, you can tell them the "right" answer and feel that you have done your job, but will you have any influence on the conceptual framework of the learners? This decision to tell students the right answer yields dubious results because the learners don't have any compelling reason to change their internal conceptual framework based on teacher comments.

A student's understanding about school science may be at odds with his or her experience. Students may have "school knowledge." This is the knowledge set students absorb and regurgitate for the test and then forget. They also have their real-world knowledge. This is the knowledge they fall back on outside of school to address their world. This knowledge is based in their life experience. A student's understanding of these two knowledge sets may never have been tested in any real way. It's also likely that the relationship between these two knowledge sets is completely unexamined.

The *Reading: How do my ideas compare with others?* phase of the SWH sets the stage for the learner to compare and examine these knowledge sets. Students consider the value of their ideas with experts as well as classmates. At this stage, negotiation for meaning around the big ideas is encouraged to continue internally and also promoted as social negotiation with others.

Remember these words from Chapter 2?

> What does it mean to interact with this knowledge? Cognitive theories of learning are based on the notion that a learner has to negotiate meaning, that is, a learner has his or her own knowledge that will interact with the new knowledge to increase the total amount of knowledge stored. The learner has to negotiate with himself or herself on the individual level and across the various groups of people that he or she will interact with daily. For example, when studying force the student has to negotiate what he or she understands about the word, negotiate what meaning the teacher in the science classroom brings to the word, and negotiate with family members and with peers when in after-school activities. In each of these contexts, the meaning of the word *force* can vary and the individual has to be able to negotiate a meaning of the word depending on the context. Parents can force students to "clean their bedroom," but this does not mean the teacher's concept of Newton's First Law is being applied to this act of cleaning.

The students have just come out of wrestling with their ideas and trying to assemble them into a logical and meaningful set of claims and evidence. They have worked through their ideas individually and likely through conversation with others. Think of your own learning experiences when you were trying to understand a concept that was meaningful yet quite challenging. Can you recall the internal conflict going on in your head as you tried to make sense of your ideas? At some point you hopefully felt a sense of accomplishment when the ideas began to make sense and you were able to connect the concepts into a schema or framework. At that point, a typical urge is to share your ideas with others and see if you can get some validation and, with that validation, a greater sense of confidence in your understanding. Of course, that sharing may also result in a loss of confidence and greater confusion. Either way you will continue to negotiate with yourself to make sense of the ideas and your conceptual framework. If validated, the framework strengthens and becomes more solid. If contradicted, you must as a learner decide to either remodel or abandon your unsatisfactory framework and try again to make sense of your ideas.

In this phase of the SWH approach, students share their ideas with others and compare their ideas to the ideas of others. While the SWH category's name highlights reading, a number of strategies can be used to accomplish this. These strategies include engaging in classroom discussion or conversations with experts in the field; reading from text resources such as trade books, journals, or magazines, and textbooks; and using the Internet.

Others in the classroom have just come to their own claims and evidence, which provides an opportunity for a classroom discussion. The students can present their ideas and see how they hold up under the scrutiny of their fellow students. The classroom discussion is focused on examining a student's ideas. The examination is characterized by skepticism, questions, and challenges that ultimately lead to the rejection, remodeling, or acceptance of the student's own ideas. For some students, this level of interaction will be invigorating, for others threatening, and (at least at the beginning) others will find it of little or no interest.

To establish a classroom environment that supports this kind of discussion, your focus will need to be firmly on student learning while you employ classroom management skills. The goal is to establish student-centered conversations with you as teacher participating as just another learner, not a gatekeeper that controls the discussion. Your role will be a shadowy one where you will prod other students to respond to ideas. Keep your eyes and ears open and read the group, looking for fellow students who seem to not agree with the ideas presented. Prod them publicly or privately to challenge the ideas they don't agree with. This method takes practice but is quite rewarding. If a student presents an idea that you see someone react to, encourage the public interaction with a question such as, "What do you think of that? Do you agree or disagree? Talk to them." These types of interactions will foster public negotiation and will really get at the point of what others think about the ideas.

If students are presenting their findings to the large group or to another small group, ask students to record notes while the other group(s) are presenting their findings. This graphic organizer in Figure 7.1 is one example of a way to structure note taking.

Students may create a T-chart to capture similarities and differences among the various claims and evidence presented by other student groups. Students may also use journals or notebooks to keep track of their ideas and the ideas of others.

Classroom management is critical to establish an environment where it is safe for students to share their own ideas and challenge the ideas of others. Maintain control of the atmosphere with ground rules that keep the discussion focused on ideas not on persons. The debate of ideas should be encouraged—this debate can be very vigorous as long as it stays on ideas. Any idea should be fair game for debate and everyone must work under the tenet of having to defend any idea that they put forth in the public setting. You know that any interactions that create an unsafe atmosphere and make people feel small or stupid will shut down the healthy debate of ideas. Here you must be sure and strong to prevent any unhealthy exchanges. The emphasis is on the public negotiation, and the ultimate responsibility for the creation of the atmosphere is yours.

As debating their own ideas becomes common practice, even those students who seem uninterested in the process will become engaged. Primarily because they've had an opportunity to wrestle with their own claims and evidence, students will have something to share rather than straight regurgitation. For others in the reluctant category, the "realness" of the dialogue will draw them in as they recognize that it's not just another activity that tries to tell them how to think.

# SWH Tool

**Figure 7.1.**  *Graphic organizer for note taking with group*

| Group Member: | Claim: (usually one sentence) | Evidence: (bullet what you think is significant) | Questions: (what about the strength of their evidence still bothers you?) |
|---|---|---|---|
|  |  |  |  |
|  |  |  |  |
|  |  |  |  |
|  |  |  |  |
|  |  |  |  |

The in-class debate can also be expanded to include "experts." Invite experts into the class to join in the discussion. When you do this, remember they are experts on the big ideas while you are the expert on teaching and learning. Set guidelines for the experts just as you do with the class. Explain that they are to be participants, not lecturers, and that they need to follow the class guidelines.

If experts aren't available or it isn't practical or timely to bring them into the classroom, then take the classroom to them. The use of technology can connect students and experts from all around the world. Email conversations work, as do the real-time chat opportunities. Have students find eminent experts in the field of the big ideas and then have them offer their ideas to the experts for feedback. The real issue is selecting the technology medium that best serves the purpose of the negotiation. Don't let the technology get in the way.

Another strategy for seeing what others think about student ideas is to provide a wide range of written materials that allow the students to read what others are saying about their ideas. Try going to the library and selecting all the books, periodicals, newspapers, and other materials you can find on your concepts and check them out to your classroom. Load up a cart with the materials and roll them into the classroom. Supplement the library books with textbooks from your classroom. You can get a great supply of single copybooks from the publishers to review. Add your college books to the list if you have any. You might as well get some good out of those textbooks you kept and didn't sell back at pennies on the dollar.

Students can use these materials to find what others are saying about their ideas. Teachers practicing the SWH approach have found that students ask to go to the textbooks and read about their ideas. Do you often have students asking to read their text?

The act of reading moves to a more private form of negotiation and can make your job of assessing student progress in the negotiation process a bit more challenging. Later in the chapter, you'll read more about the Reflection stage of the SWH and how it can help in this assessment. Using reading strategies can also help students make meaning from text. As students use the strategies, it provides you an opportunity to listen to student dialogue or results in the creation of a written product that can be used to assess student progress.

A variety of reading strategies can be used to help students make meaning from the text. Graphic organizers can be used to help structure note taking. If students have been using a KWL or concept map, they may add to it as they read. It may be helpful for students to use a different color to represent ideas they gleaned from reading. They may also use note-taking guides. The following example promotes the idea of using multiple sources as well as provides a purpose for reading as students focus on their questions. It also provides an easy way to compare the findings from the different sources as students look for patterns and relationships.

# SWH Tool

**Figure 7.2.** *Data chart for note taking*

## Data Chart for Note Taking

| Your Name and Topic | Question #1 | Question #2 | Question #3 |
|---|---|---|---|
| Source #1 | Answer to Question #1 from Source #1 | Answer to Question #2 from Source #1 | Answer to Question #3 from Source #1 |
| Source #2 | Answer to Question #1 from Source #2 | Answer to Question #2 from Source #2 | Answer to Question #3 from Source #2 |
| Source #3 | Answer to Question #1 from Source #3 | Answer to Question #2 from Source #3 | Answer to Question #3 from Source #3 |

Students may use various summarizing frames such as the argumentation frame (Marzano, Gaddy, & Dean, 2000), proposition/support outline (Billmeyer, 2004), or problem/solution frame (Marzano, Gaddy, & Dean, 2000). Each frame includes guiding questions that students use as they read. After reading and taking notes around the questions, students summarize the text in their own words. The questions associated with these three summarizing frames follow.

### *Argumentation Frame* (adapted from Marzano, Gaddy, and Dean, 2000)

1. What information is being presented that leads to a claim?
2. What claim does the author make about the problem or situation?
3. What examples or explanations does the author present to support the claim?
4. What restrictions or explanations does the author present to support his or her claim?

### *Proposition/Support Outline* (adapted from Billmeyer, 2004)

Topic:

Proposition (Claim):

1. What evidence or information is presented that leads to the claim?
2. What expert authority does the author cite to lend credibility to his or her claims and evidence?
3. What logic or reasoning does the author present to support this claim?

### *Problem/Solution Frame* (adapted from Marzano, Gaddy, & Dean, 2000)

1. What is the problem?
2. What is a possible solution?
   a. What are the risks and benefits for this solution?
3. What is another possible solution?
   a. What are the risks and benefits for this solution?
4. What is another possible solution?
   a. What are the risks and benefits for this solution?

Text examples can provide students with high-quality models of what a "good" argument looks like. From these models, students can improve their own skills at constructing arguments. As students develop their own skills, they will also become more skeptical readers and question the author and his or her claims and evidence.

As described earlier in the book in Chapter 3, *we need to plan opportunities for both public and private negotiation about the relationship between new information and the big ideas of science.* As teachers, we need to know what the students are doing with the new information. How are they connecting what we have shared with them to what they currently believe about the topic? Just because we give information does not mean that students will store the information in the manner in which we intended. This step in the SWH process allows for public negotiation and creates a situation for students to wrestle with the strength of their ideas on conceptual frameworks in a private manner as well.

# Reflecting and Considering How Ideas Have Changed

The last phase of the SWH is *Reflection: How have my ideas changed?* Reflection is part of many classrooms and is often incorporated into lessons. The reflection process that is practiced is often not as productive as it could be in that it doesn't get deep enough into the learning process to provide the strongest opportunity for learning. The most powerful learning opportunity includes not only reflection on *what* new ideas have emerged but also contemplating *how* those ideas emerged as students think about their own thinking, or metacognition. This final step of the SWH approach provides a powerful opportunity for the learners. As part of the reflection, students ask themselves these types of questions:

1. What were my ideas prior to the SWH?
2. What were my ideas after the SWH?
3. How have they been changed?
4. What caused my ideas to change?

This seems like a straightforward and simple task, but it doesn't always work out that way with the students. Early attempts at this process in classrooms using the SWH produced student responses that included:

❖ My ideas haven't changed.

❖ My ideas have changed. I thought the answer to my question would be that the cells in the shallow water would be the same as in the deep water. (A freshwater cell unit)

These reflections don't show any real depth in the students' awareness of the big ideas. Nor do they show how the students' conceptual frameworks have changed to incorporate new ideas. Getting students to be aware of what is going on in their heads can be a bit of a challenge. No one may have ever cared before about how they as individual students were learning and what was going on inside their heads. In the past, only external products may have been valued.

To get students to become more aware of their learning, you can go back to the concept map. Have them do a post-SWH map and compare that map to their original. This can be a small-group project where the students can work on their maps together and then discuss the changes. This task creates an opportunity to see how others' maps have changed in comparison to their own map. Students can talk about their learning as well as reflect as individuals. This process will likely focus on "what" students learned.

Students may also be asked to provide feedback in the form of peer assessment on written products. The ground rules for classroom discourse can guide the ground rules for written comments. Stay on the idea level and keep comments away from personal attack. Consider the following vignette:

> When the class got their work back with comments from seventh graders one of the students was moved to tears. The tears didn't come from a poor grade. The work received a good grade. No, she was hurt by the comments from the seventh grader, comments from a real person, her words, not teacher comments. She had invested herself into the work and felt a very personal effect from the feedback.

The nature of the peer comments received by this student was honest and positive. What is clear in the vignette is how vested students can become in their work through the SWH. The challenge for the teacher is to establish an environment where students welcome feedback.

The next level of reflection is to increase the metacognitive awareness of the students in reflection. Getting the students to think about their own thinking will strengthen their sense of control of their learning and, in doing so, increase the students' level of confidence in their own learning process. Students might use a quick-write in response to a question such as:

**1.** What did you, your team members, or the teacher do to help you learn?

**2.** What activities were most helpful to your learning process and why?

**3.** What activities were least helpful to your learning process and why?

Another strategy to help students develop metacognitive skills is to have conversations with your students about your learning process as you move through the SWH process. Talk about your learning process with the class as a model of thinking about thinking—called a "thinkaloud." Through the thinkaloud, make specific connections to reading from a text, then unpacking your thinking about the text and how you make sense of the text. Also describe ways in which the text promotes ideas that may be consistent with your thinking and also ways in which the text challenges your ideas.

Plan a regular time to discuss this process with the class, and in the discussion ask your students to become active partners in your learning process. Use your metacognitive reflections as an example for students who will likely have a simple, undeveloped concept of reflection. Students also need to appreciate the hard work involved in metacognitive processes.

Using nonclassroom examples based on student interests may help as well. You might use athletics, cooking, car repair, or other personal interests. If you have a class that is interested in video games, have them reflect on how they learn to play the game. Many video games have multiple levels that must be completed successfully before players can move to the next level. Some learning process is involved with moving past sticking points in the player's progress. How does a player progress? Have students try talking through their process. They will most likely talk about an analysis of the situation causing the block, assessment of the play process that is currently being used, and development of a strategy to become successful. This experience provides practice at reflection. It also provides an opportunity to highlight elements of learning that we want them to employ in learning science.

The first efforts of students in the Reflection phase often produce simple answers that aren't insightful regarding their learning. The old rules of regurgitating the bits of information in just the right form have a strong influence on students as you try to change your classroom atmosphere. Changing this response will take time. Students are not used to really examining their learning and thinking about what goes on in their head when learning science. Guidance will have to be provided and this will take skilled questions. Consider the following sample Reading section:

Student Voice 1
The experts agree with my ideas.

Student Voice 2
My own and my group's ideas compare very similarly to what the experts say. The only thing that was a bit different was that they just had more information and had a better idea about rockets.

Student Voice 3
Before reading: I think that on my rocket I need small triangular fins. My rocket needs sturdy fins that don't flop around easily, or else it's like having no fins, which won't go far. The bigger fins will create more drag so it won't go far because drag is like friction but in the air. We should also put the fins on the back of the rockets.

After reading: I still think the same thing except now not only do my fins need to be small and triangular but smooth, thin, stiff, and lightweight, too.

These three reading sections are from the same lab experience but were written by three different students. The first is a common beginning response to the Reading prompt. Often students will simply write, "My ideas haven't changed." As you progress through Students 2 and 3 you see more insight into their thinking. And with Student 3 a picture of how her understanding has changed is showing through in her writing. With Student 3 the teacher asked the student how the ideas were the same or different. Student 2 says in his work, "The only thing . . . " This shows he sees his ideas have changed but doesn't really talk about "why" when he says the experts have more information and better ideas. As the teacher, we would want to ask questions about why they say this.

Increased metacognition, or thinking about thinking, strips away the notion of the teacher as the gatekeeper and controller of learning. Control of learning reinforces students' awareness of their own learning process. This awareness removes the mystique of learning that teachers often perpetuate with a classroom where the information is carefully controlled and meted out on an apparent need-to-know basis. Such an atmosphere leaves the student in the dark and results in passivity on the part of the learners. As students become more in tune with what works for them as learners, they are more able to help create this kind of environment for themselves. Alternatively, as students stretch their minds through other kinds of activities, they become more flexible in their ability to learn in a variety of environments and through many strategies.

Skillful use of the Reflection portion of the SWH strips away the mystery of learning and creates a classroom atmosphere that is characterized by learners who are active partners in the learning. The teacher becomes a cooperative colleague with students where all are working toward a common goal in the classroom where this change is realized at a high level. Does that describe your current classroom? You have often been given the charge to create lifetime learners. To create lifetime learners, empower them today and pull them into the learning process. Get your students to accept the responsibility of being in control of their learning as active partners.

In the learning chapter the idea of learning includes the idea: The learner has to negotiate with himself or herself on the individual level and across the various groups of people that he or she will interact with daily. Reading and Reflection lead to this. If your students' ideas and new conceptual frameworks are scrutinized by both the student and others, the student will either see support of their ideas or they will see the weaknesses in their claims or the evidence. When weaknesses appear, the student can then revise the framework as the one in control—*only the learner can manage this process.*

## Teacher's Voice

I was surprised how difficult the Reflection part of the SWH was. The Reading seemed to come easily to the class. They wanted to know what everyone thought about their ideas. The amazing part was their openness in the process. They would ask classmates about their ideas, read the textbook, and ask me. If any or all of these sources of feedback didn't match their claim and evidence, they would easily discount all of the feedback. They held on to their ideas with tenacity. The argument that ensued was incredible. I was pleasantly surprised to find that in the pursuit of "What others think" the class would ask everyone in the class about their results. When disagreement occurred a heated debate would ensue. I didn't have to be involved at all. I was so excited to have real debate going spontaneously. The only source that went unchallenged was emails to experts. The class would find the world experts and email them to get their position. They would listen to the "experts" and accept them without challenge. I find this amazing and a bit frightening.

This atmosphere of debate and challenging others didn't transfer easily to the SWH. I think I struggled so much because this is so foreign to both the students and me. I just wasn't used to digging into what the learners thought about their learning and apparently neither were they. I was constantly frustrated by their early SWH responses to Reflection. I would get the answer "My ideas haven't changed" way too often. I didn't get a good result on the Reflection piece until I scored the SWH based totally on the Reflection piece. Once we broke through, the Reflection began to improve. That indicates to me that the problem wasn't ability; the problem was either discomfort or unwillingness. I scored an SWH with the entire grade based on Reflection and wouldn't score the SWH until they actually had done Reflection. Once they broke through and started to reflect they made the connection between the Reflection piece and their taking responsibility and control of their learning.

A theme running throughout this text is that the learner has to negotiate with himself or herself on the individual level and across the various groups of people that he or she will interact with. The Reading and Reflection phases of the SWH provide another opportunity for this kind of learning experience. Student ideas must be scrutinized by both the student generating the idea and others so that the resulting conceptual framework is more consistent with the existing scientific knowledge base around the big ideas of science.

## SWH Student Example Progression

The following three SWH samples represent what you might see from a student in a tenth-grade ecology class. The samples represent the changes that can be seen in a student's performance as he or she moves through multiple trials of using the SWH. These are adapted from a classroom where the teacher and the students were new to the SWH approach.

# First SWH Student Example—Part 1

*Beginning Ideas: What questions do I have?*

Are the biomes the same?

*Tests: What did I do? (How did you test to answer your question?)*

Observe posters of the different biomes and compare them. Look for some of the important factors of each.

*Observations: What did I find? (What did you find when you tested?)*

Many of the biomes have similar characteristics but not all the same values of these characteristics. They also do not all have the same group of characteristics.

*Claims: What inferences can I make? (Explain what you think happened.)*

No, I don't think that the biomes are the same.

*Evidence: How do I know?*

I think this because they all have many different values of properties. The grasslands have an annual precipitation of 50–100 cm, unlike the desert with less than 50 cm of precipitation annually. They all have different forms of life. The tundra has shrubs and sedges, while the taiga has pine trees. They also have very different temperatures. The tundra has a range of temperatures of –30 degrees to 54 degrees Fahrenheit, from its coldest season to its warmest season. The rain forest has a range of temperatures of 77–88 degrees Fahrenheit. These values make a lot of difference to what biome you are talking about.

*Reading: How do my ideas compare with others?*

The book says small differences in temperature or precipitation can create many different biomes. The book is saying that small differences can change the kind of biome. By this sentence it is also saying that the biomes are not the same. A lot of the people in my class also answered no. They had a lot of the same reasons I did.

*Reflection: How have my ideas changed?*

I learned what some of the main characteristics are of biomes. I know a little about each of the biomes, and what certain characteristics each one has. I learned a lot because I didn't even know what a biome was before.

This first student SWH example has the appearance of being quality work. It matches the standard that is used in evaluating standard lab write-ups. Upon closer inspection the work is shallow and of a reporting nature. Good, solid argumentation is lacking. The question does not lead the student to an open-ended search for answers to the questions. Instead the work has every appearance of a standard report on biomes. The science language for the chapter is scattered through the report but really doesn't indicate understanding. For the first SWH this is very standard. Now have a look at a second effort.

## First SWH Student Example—Part 2

*Beginning Ideas: What questions do I have?*

What is the relationship between matter and energy?

*Tests: What did I do? (How did you test to answer your question?)*

I read the text of the book and took notes on it.

*Observations: What did I find? (What did you find when you tested?)*

I found that matter and energy are alike. They are both distributed throughout an ecosystem, but they aren't distributed the same way.

*Claims: What inferences can I make? (Explain what you think happened.)*

I think that matter depends on energy.

*Evidence: How do I know?*

Energy is the beginning of the food chain. Energy is in the form of sunlight in the beginning of the food chain. All of the organisms need energy to live. Plants use energy for photosynthesis and to grow. Some organisms called herbivores depend on the plants for food. Other organisms called carnivores depend on the animals for food. All these organisms are depending on the energy from the sunlight because they are depending on one another. All this matter is depending on energy.

*Reading: How do my ideas compare with others?*

The book says energy is the fuel of life, which shows that everything depends on it. If there was no energy there wouldn't be any matter.

*Reflection: How have my ideas changed?*

I now know what biomes and ecosystems depend on. I also know what keeps them going and some of the main characteristics. I learned how the food chains start. I learned how energy moves through the ecosystem.

The second attempt at the SWH by this student again reads like a classic report. The big ideas aren't driving this SWH. The recitation of facts is the focus. This is a typical SWH from students who have likely been successful in the typical classroom and are depending on what got them ahead in the school game. The SWH lacks any personality and doesn't show a high level of student engagement and excitement. Growth will usually start to show up in the Claims and Evidence. This shows a better evidence section than the first example. The SWH components may have been present but they don't jump off the page at you as the reader. You have surely read many reports just like this one.

## First SWH Student Example—Part 3

*Beginning Ideas: What questions do I have?*

> What is the leading cause of water pollution?
>
> What are some of the effects of water pollution?
>
> How can you prevent water pollution?

*Tests: What did I do? (How did you test to answer your question?)*

> I researched my question on the Internet.

*Observations: What did I find? (What did you find when you tested?)*

> I found that there is one major cause of water pollution, many effects, and a few ways to prevent it.

*Claims: What inferences can I make? (Explain what you think happened.)*

> The leading cause of water pollution is nonpoint source pollution. A major effect is that many animals and fish can die. One way to prevent water pollution is to clean up after yourself.

*Evidence: How do I know?*

> Nonpoint source pollution is also known as polluted runoff. Seventy percent of America's harmed waterways are impaired because of pollution from nonpoint sources. It comes from many natural and human-made pollutants. Some of the sources are urban streets and lawns, highways, forests, parking lots, faulty septic systems, factories, and agricultural lands. Lawns and agricultural lands may contain excess fertilizers, animal wastes, herbicides, and insecticides. Streets, highways, parking lots, and factories may have oil, grease, and toxic chemicals. All these things cause water pollution. As surface water moves across and through the land it picks up and carries away these pollutants. It takes them to lakes, rivers, wetlands, coastal waters, and even underground sources of drinking water.
>
> One effect of water pollution is animals and fish die. This is because the excess fertilizers and animals' wastes are being carried to lakes and rivers. This causes algal blooms, or excessive growth of algae, because there is a sudden availability of nutrients. This takes the oxygen from the surrounding waters. As the algae die, they take needed oxygen from the water.
>
> As you already know, many things cause pollution. So in order to prevent pollution, you have to do things that don't cause it. So instead of littering,

throw your trash away. Also, don't overfertilize. Another major issue is chemicals. One way to prevent chemical pollution in water is to make treatment ponds to settle the pollution before it gets to rivers.

*Reading: How do my ideas compare with others?*

I agree with the book where it says water pollution degrades aquatic habitats in streams, rivers, lakes, and oceans.

*Reflection: How have my ideas changed?*

I now know what the major cause of water pollution is. I also found out what some of the effects are and how to prevent them.

This third example shows no improvement in the grasp of the big issues and getting at these ideas. Each of the attempts demonstrates a high-achieving student hanging on to what has always worked in the past. From the teacher's perspective, the first place to analyze these SWH attempts is the question. Do these questions get at big ideas and issues that students want to discover or are they just points in a curriculum with facts attached? In the early implementation stages it may help to focus on just one piece of the SWH at a time, beginning with the questions. Then build on the process to create a sense in the students that their job is to identify their questions and answer them based on evidence that is used to build a meaningful claim. These three attempts represent what teachers often see when they are early in implementation of the SWH. Old habits die hard and students will hang onto their existing conceptualizations about school just as they will about content.

Change takes time. To produce growth you as teacher need to guide your students and not accept the status quo. If the work doesn't measure up, don't accept it and insist that it be done well.

The next sample set is representative of a teacher who has had more experience with the SWH.

## Second SWH Student Example—Part 1

*Beginning Ideas: What questions do I have?*

Which ramp is less work, less power, and saves the most energy while pushing a wheelchair?

*Tests: What did I do? (How did you test to answer your question?)*

❖ Use binders, books, and wood to make the ramps

❖ Tie a piece of string to the car to pull it up

❖ Put a weight in the back of the car and tape it in so it won't fall out

❖ Attach the spring scale to the string and pull the car up the ramp

❖ Time how long it takes to pull car up the ramp

❖ Record time

❖ Repeat steps 4–6 with other ramp

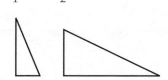

1    2

#2 because it would could go faster and use less work than #1.

*Observations: What did I find? (What did you find when you tested?)*

| Trial # | Distance (cm) | Force (N) fast | Force (N) slow | Time (sec) fast | Time (sec) slow |
|---------|---------------|----------------|----------------|-----------------|-----------------|
| Ramp 1–1 | 36 | 1.8 | 1.5 | 2.31 | 10.72 |
| Ramp 1–2 | 36 | 2 | 2 | 2.85 | 7.94 |
| Ramp 1–3 | 36 | 2.1 | 1.5 | 2.80 | 11.2 |
| Ramp 2–1 | 81 | 2 | 1.8 | 2.28 | 6.56 |
| Ramp 2–2 | 81 | 2 | 1.5 | 2.44 | 4.93 |
| Ramp 2–3 | 81 | 1.9 | 1.5 | 2.47 | 6.53 |

|  | Distance | Force | Time | Steep |
|--|----------|-------|------|-------|
| **Average** |  |  |  |  |
| 36 cm | 1.96 N | 1.7N | 2.65 sec | 9.95 sec |
| **Long** |  |  |  |  |
| 81 cm | 1.96 N | 1.6 N | 2.39 sec | 6 sec |
|  | Fast | Slow | Fast | Slow |

*Claims: What inferences can I make? (Explain what you think happened.)*

Based on our experiment we would recommend using the longer ramp because you can go faster and use less power than with the steep ramp.

*Evidence: How do I know?*

We know that the longer ramp is better because it averaged only 6 seconds and only used 1.6 Newtons, whereas the steep ramp averaged nearly 10 seconds and used 1.7 Newtons of force.

*Reading: How do my ideas compare with others?*

*Reflection: How have my ideas changed?*

> My original claim was: Use the big ramp because it will take less energy and work to get up it because it's not as steep. After doing the experiment, I have concluded that the steep ramp actually takes *less* work and power than the long ramp, because the steep work was 0.7 J and the long ramp was 1.5 J/s, and the steep power was only 0.1 J/s whereas the long ramp power was 0.4 J/s.
>
> Work and power are different by how they are calculated. Work = force × distance and Power = work ÷ time.
>
> I know that work is applying force to something to move it a distance, and power is the rate at which you do work.

This SWH represents a high-level student who is a successful student as well. The example represents a high vocabulary but lacks in the argumentation that is used in the Claims and Evidence sections. The Evidence section is not as strong as the rest of the work. The Reflection section does show an insight into the changing process of what was in the student's head and how the SWH helped shift his or her concepts. The student is working around the big ideas here and it shows. The next sample would be what you could expect in May.

## Second SWH Student Example—Part 2

*Beginning Ideas: What questions do I have?*

> How do we make a balloon float without helium?

*Tests: What did I do? (How did you test to answer your question?)*

> First the five of us went and got all our supplies. Then we formed the wire into a circle to make the base of the balloon. While that is going on, we also cut and folded the tissue paper to make the actual balloon. After that we taped the tissue paper together to make the actual balloon and glued and taped the balloon to the wire. We did a check for holes and fixed any that were found. After construction we tested the balloon.

*Observations: What did I find? (What did you find when you tested?)*

> Our first attempt was without success. It was a windy day, but that really wasn't a problem. After getting the canister lit, we placed the balloon over it, and watched while it gradually filled up with hot air. Even though it filled up it still couldn't get into the air. We concluded then that our balloon was too small (in volume) and too heavy. We kept the same general design for our second try, but made the balloon part a lot bigger and lighter by using an actual pattern for the

balloon. We also decided to use stick glue instead of tape to decrease the weight. When finished, our balloon looked like a giant onion, which is how it got its name, La Cebolla ("the onion" in Spanish). Anyway we then tried for the second time. It worked better, and filled with lots of hot air but still couldn't get into the air. It looked a little lopsided, so we're trying to fix this. We also noticed some holes that needed fixing, so these were one reason that it couldn't get off the ground as those holes let the hot air escape. We did have a very good heat source though.

*Claims: What inferences can I make? (Explain what you think happened.)*

Volume, less density, heat, lighter materials.

You need a balloon that is very lightweight and that has a huge, huge volume so that it has plenty of room for the hot air molecules to spread out and start bouncing around. Your balloon should be gargantuan compared to your heat source so that the molecules can speed up and spread out.

*Evidence: How do I know?*

I know first of all that the balloon has to be really light in weight. I know this because if it weighs too much then no matter how big it is, it still won't get off the ground because it is too heavy. I also know that the balloon has to be really big in volume, because the first try was too small and so the hot air particles couldn't spread out enough. The second try (which was bigger) filled up, and looked like it might float but still wasn't big enough. Our actual balloon needed to be a lot bigger because even though the particles were speeding up and spreading out, there just wasn't enough room plus there were some holes, so that didn't help either.

*Reading: How do my ideas compare with others?*

I think we were right on track with our second try. I thought we had a good design: It wasn't too heavy, but was just not quite big enough. A lot of other balloons were very simple but ended up being too heavy. Many of the others had strings attached to them but I didn't see the significance of the string and actually think it got in the way. I think if we had worked a little more carefully on that second try and found the holes and realized the lopsidedness before the launch, it might have made a slight difference.

*Reflection: How have my ideas changed?*

At first I just thought of a hot air balloon like this: The heat goes into balloon, balloon rises. Obviously I was wrong. It's more like this: get BIG balloon, small heat source, heat goes up into balloon, hot air particles speed up a lot and spread out, which makes the balloon float into the air. I didn't realize how big a role volume and density played in a hot air balloon. I already knew that it had to be really light but now I know that the balloon has to be big enough in volume to make the particles spread out and make the air in the balloon less dense so it can get into the air.

In this SWH the writer gives a much better picture into his or her grasp of the big ideas. The concept of density is at the center and from the Reflection piece you can see the change in the learner's understanding and where he or she still could use more experiences to sharpen conceptual understanding.

## Assessing the SWH

One issue that hasn't been specifically addressed is that of grades. How does the SWH approach fit into your grading system? The SWH process can create opportunities for grading and products for scoring. Scoring the SWH experience should reflect a focus on students' development of conceptual understanding and a richer conceptual framework. Scoring would likely take place more on the Claims, Evidence, and Reflection phases of the SWH. Students may also be involved in peer assessment and self-assessment to help students develop the skills necessary to move through the heuristic successfully.

As you implement the approach and students are not familiar with the expectations you can focus on the individual pieces of the templates to help the students increase their ability to operate within the argumentation system of the SWH. If questions are a struggle for students, emphasize the questions in the scoring process first. Consider weighting the questions more heavily so the students will focus on developing quality questions. After the class has developed an understanding of the value and structure of good questions you can work down through the SWH, emphasizing the various stages of the SWH in the scoring. Continue on this way until the students can work within the SWH without the heuristic itself being a problem.

The evaluation can be used by both the students for self-evaluation and by the teacher for SWH evaluation. As discussed earlier the values assigned for each box can vary. In the scenario of developing an increased student ability in the questions section, you may score the question section at 1–3 for needs work, 4–6 for making progress, 7–9 for almost there, and 10–12 for very good. The rest of the sections could be scored on a 1-, 2-, 3-, and 4-point value for each progression across the scale. That would create a total value for the SWH of 36 points. Teachers have even focused so much on a section the students were struggling with that they only scored that portion of the SWH. This can also cut the amount of work for scoring the SWH.

# SWH Tool

**Figure 7.3.** *SWH evaluation form*

| SWH Evaluation Form | | Needs Work | Making Progress | Almost There | Very Good |
|---|---|---|---|---|---|
| Questions | Questions are testable<br>More complex answer needed than yes or no | | | | |
| Tests | Tests are appropriate for questions | | | | |
| Observations | Data was recorded accurately<br>All possible observations were made | | | | |
| Claims | Claim is appropriate for the questions<br>Claim is derived from observation<br>Claim is concise | | | | |
| Evidence | Comes from observation<br>Logically supports the claim | | | | |
| Reading | Multiple sources are used to compare my claims and evidence against | | | | |
| Reflections | Explains why their beginning ideas have or have not changed | | | | |
| Writing | Correct spelling and complete sentences<br>Ideas are presented such that the reader can easily understand them | | | | |

A teacher who was having trouble getting quality work from the students on their SWH write-ups used the evaluation process to raise the students' conceptualization of what a quality SWH should look like. The students were given an SWH along with an evaluation form. Their assignment was to evaluate the SWH.

The evaluation process for the SWH experience needs to be aligned with the new classroom practices. The SWH approach is all about changing the students' conceptual framework and helping students get at the big ideas of the unit. The evaluation needs to be based on students' increased conceptual understanding of the big ideas of science. If your classroom evaluations have been based on questions that get at facts, you will need to begin to use conceptual questions. Conceptual questions need to be open-ended and allow the students to communicate their new conceptual understanding.

With the pressure to have students increase their standardized test scores, conceptual questions can seem out of place and not all that helpful. More than other types of questions, they will allow you to see what is happening with your students' learning. The conceptual questions for your units can be based on your standards and benchmarks. If the nature of questions on your standardized assessment raises concerns with shifting away from more fact-based questions and toward more conceptual questions, check out Chapter 10 for reassurance that students' performance will actually increase on standardized tests through effective use of the SWH and conceptual questions.

If the SWH approach is about big ideas, classroom assessment needs to also switch to the big ideas. The change you are attempting in your classroom is based upon understanding learning and teaching and the role the SWH process can play in the learning process. At each step of the process, be diligent in checking your classroom, your teaching, and your learners' behavior against your heightened awareness of teaching in the service of learning.

## Revisiting the Big Idea

Reading and Reflection followed by classroom evaluation of the SWH are tools of classroom negotiation that allow learners to sharpen their conceptual understanding of the big ideas of your unit. This chapter has been all about negotiation: negotiation with self, others, experts, and you as teacher. Keep this in mind as you work through the SWH approach and encourage your students and yourself to be aware of this negotiation process and view the classroom interactions through that lens. Openly discuss what is happening at the conceptual level in terms of your big ideas and what is happening at the metacognitive level with the learners. As you and your students understand what is happening in your own heads, you become more powerful learners who can transfer these learning skills to new circumstances in life. This completes the SWH section, but this is not the end of the SWH process. Much of the richness of the process follows with writing experiences and conceptual evaluation. A variety of ways to complete your SWH unit are discussed in the following chapter.

# CHAPTER 8

# Wrapping Up an SWH Unit

## The Summary-Writing Experience

W e have discussed in the previous chapters how to use the SWH. However, how do we shape the conclusion to a unit of work? Having done three or four SWH activities, how do you as the teacher tie everything together? Should you get the students to do a chapter summary and answer the end-of-chapter questions? We would suggest that there is a need to continue to use the writing-to-learn experiences that you have started with the SWH approach. There is a need to get students to try to link all their thinking that emerged during the inquiry experiences. If we want to promote the big ideas of the topic and encourage students to examine their conceptual understanding, we must give them an opportunity to explain what they have learned.

We have encouraged the use of writing-to-learn strategies as a critical method for promoting learning. Our research over the last ten years has shown that students who use these strategies have been more successful when answering test questions than students who do not. We have tried a variety of different types of writing across a range of classroom settings, and each time students have had success in gaining greater understanding of the topic.

## Sequence of a Unit

The basic outline for a unit is shown in Figure 8.1. This sequence is very broad but does highlight the essential dimensions of the unit and how we see the flow of the unit going.

As can be seen from this sequence, we have placed importance on some form of summary-writing experience. Building from the description of writing-to-learn strategies presented in Chapter 4, we believe that this summary-writing activity is important

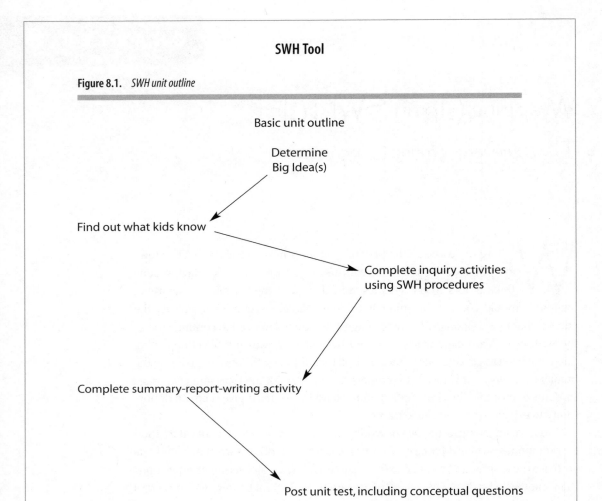

**Figure 8.1.** *SWH unit outline*

Basic unit outline

Determine
Big Idea(s)

Find out what kids know

Complete inquiry activities
using SWH procedures

Complete summary-report-writing activity

Post unit test, including conceptual questions

and is not simply writing down the chapter summary in the book or copying the summary written down on the blackboard by the teacher. While the writing activities associated with the individual SWH experiences serve a vital function, the writing in the summary experience serves an equally vital but different function.

## SWH Summary-Writing Experience

The writing that the students do in completing each SWH investigation is focused on building argument. The students are trying to frame a scientific argument through writing by answering the questions on the various sections of Questions, Procedure, Observations, Claims, Evidence, Reading, and Reflection. The purpose of the writing is for the students to link these various components together. Through their writing the students are required to ensure that their claim is based on their questions (if it is not, then they need to change their question to match their claim), that their observations are framed in a logical reasoned manner when they put forward their evidence for their claim, confirm their data and evidence from checking with other sources, reviews and makes a comment on the claims and evidence they have generated, and finally, that the reflection section does examine if and how their ideas have changed.

The focus of the writing is on a particular activity. Thus, over the course of a unit, the student is required to complete three, four, or five of these types of write-ups. While the flow of the unit is about seeing each activity as connected—that is, the question for the second SWH generally arises from the first SWH, and so on—each write-up is viewed as separate from the other. Thus, *each write-up is intended to structure an argument for the activity and to build conceptual understanding from that activity*. The question becomes, what type of activity will help students link all of the SWH activities together?

The purpose of the summary-writing experience is to link the SWH activities together. We would emphasize that this writing is different from the SWH type of writing that the students complete. How? The difference is in the purpose for the writing. As explained previously, the purpose of the writing for each SWH is to build a science argument; however, the purpose of the summary-writing experience is to link the conceptual ideas dealt with in the SWH activities together. That is, *the writing is intended to help students link the concepts that are being dealt with in the topic together, to build the conceptual framework for, and hence understanding of, the topic*.

When we talk about a summary-writing experience we are talking about using more diversified types of writing as outlined in Chapter 4. We have had students write travel brochures, letters to the editor, explanations to younger children, and newspaper articles for the general public. All of our research has shown that we need to have students write to peers or to a younger audience. Every time students write to the teacher or an older student audience, they want to use big words, that is, they want to use the vocabulary words without explaining what these are. They use the words as labels and pretend that they understand what those words mean. Having to write to a younger audience means that they cannot simply use the big words. They have to explain what these words mean, and this is where the value of the writing activity lies. The students are required to go through a number of different translations of the science language. As can be seen from the diagram in Figure 8.2, students translate the science language for themselves—as the science language is presented the students are constantly trying to attach meaning to it. The only vocabulary that they

**Figure 8.2.** *The language relationship*

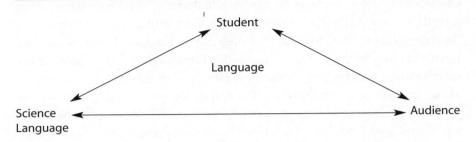

Dynamic relationship between science language, student, and audience.

have to make meaning for is what they know about science. Thus, they try to build understanding from what they know to what they do not know. Having filtered the science through their own understanding, the students are then required to translate the science for their audience. Instead of simply giving the labels back to the teachers, they are now required to write the science in a way in which their younger audience or peers can begin to understand.

Finally, the students then have to answer questions on the test in terms of the science language used in the topic. They are now required to translate back into the official science language. This constant movement between these different forms of the same language means that students constantly have to deal with the concepts of the topic in a much richer and more meaningful way than trying to remember simply a list of vocabulary words.

## Getting Started with Summary Writing

In referring back to Chapter 4, there is a need to determine the writing type, purpose, audience, and topic for the piece of writing. As the teacher you need to make decisions regarding what you believe the students are comfortable with and what you want to attempt to achieve as the end point of the unit. The summary-writing activity is the final piece in the unit before assessing the students. We would point out that in all of our research studies we have asked the teachers not to give practice questions to the students who are using the summary-report-writing exercise. We believe that by asking students to deal with the underlying concepts of the topic we can promote better student understanding of the topic and remove the need to do practice problems.

Student #1: As I was doing it, I would think of something that would go good in it. . . . It was like I was understanding the concept as I was writing it. As I was writing, I saw that their chemical reactions influenced how they functioned. I began to understand that, but I couldn't understand how to explain it. As I was writing how diabetics' bodies function, I realize that the organisms do determine their function.

Student #2: Instead of using big words from the book such as chemical reactions or things that happen, it was kind of like going into and explaining those different things that happen. It was going in and breaking up those big words so that I could understand it piece by piece and not just writing out big words and not understanding what they mean.

Student #3: If it is a big word you have to use, like biotech regulations, you have to explain what that is. Like, you have to explain what *bio* means, what *technology* means, and *regulations* means because they don't exactly know what that is. You can't really reword it so you have to explain what every little part of what that means.

Student #4: First you dumb it down, learn that, and get the basics down really well, and then you can move on to your large textbook definitions. [You] move from the simple textbook onto the hard textbook definitions.

## Writing type

There is no right or wrong when it comes to the writing type that you want your students to use as the summary-writing experience. As we stated previously, we have used travel brochures, letters to the editor or parents, newspaper articles, textbook explanations, and cartoon strips. Our recommendation is to work with the students' English teacher and combine the assignment so that one piece of work can be marked twice—once for science content, once for English emphasis. By building this connection to English, the writing assignment can take on greater importance because science is not seen as an isolated subject. Thus, if the English teacher is working on letter writing, then ask your students to write a letter about the topic to their peers or to younger students. If you chose a newspaper article as the format for the students, we would encourage you to get a journalist or editor from the local paper to talk with the students. We have done this, resulting in the editor volunteering to review the students' work. This resulted in some of the students' work being published.

## Purpose

What are the students trying to do through the writing, apart from linking together the concepts of the topic? Are the students going to be asked to persuade, to argue a point of view, or to report? In setting the purpose for the task we need to help students understand that the purpose involved with the writing task does shape how the piece should be written. Writing a persuasive piece is different than writing a narrative. Writing a narrative is different than writing a letter. As teachers we need to help the students see that these are different and require a different structure to succeed in reaching our intended audience.

## Audience

As we have discussed, the audience should be one that requires the students to translate the science language into more everyday language. Thus, we would encourage audiences to be peers, younger audiences, parents, or the general public. Absolutely critical is for this audience to be real, that is, the audience needs to be part of the assessment process of the written piece.

## Topic

The major emphasis of the summary writing is to deal with the major ideas/concepts that have been dealt with in the unit. These ideas should have been made public throughout the unit, and, thus, in setting up the writing task these need to be reiterated. How many big ideas do you want the students to deal with in this writing: one, two, or three?

We have encouraged teachers to use this framework when outlining the summary-writing task (or any other writing task) for students. Students need to be aware that there are different demands and components of a writing task, depending on the particular choices that are made. They should realize that these are not hidden but are talked about and help them shape the writing process for them.

## Getting the Students Started

A number of different strategies can be used to get students organized and started in the writing process. We would stress again the importance of making everything transparent for the students—it will help them understand the dimensions and demands of the writing task. A number of different strategies that we have used follow:

❖ Make the concepts that you want to address clear. As a step between the SWH activities and the summary-writing piece, we would suggest the construction of a concept map. Students in small groups and/or whole-class group settings could do this. This step will enable the students to have a richer sense of the concepts that have been the focus of the unit. This concept map can then be the guiding frame for the writing task.

❖ Have a class discussion about the writing task. Outline the categories of audience, purpose, type, and topic for the students. Provide some discussion time for the students to talk with each other about what these categories mean.

❖ Allow the students in small-group settings to discuss what they need to include in their writing. Some guiding questions could be: What do they think they need to include? How do they deal with the audience? How do they shape their writing to match the writing type that has been chosen?

❖ Ask the students to outline their plans to the class as a whole, that is, what they are focusing on for their writing piece and how they are dealing with the question of the audience. This will allow for student feedback on what has been proposed. They tend to be good at discussing how the intended audience will or will not handle the science concepts that are being discussed.

❖ Outline the scoring criteria for assessing the finished product. How marks are assigned will depend on you as the teacher, but we certainly recommend that there be both science and language marks. Students need to understand that you are placing emphasis on their description of the science, how well they have followed the guidelines for the writing type, whether the writing is appropriate for the audience, and the quality of the writing in terms of flow, grammar, and punctuation.

---

**From the Students**

Student Voice #1: You have to be organized. You have . . . I mean, you can't write about something else and then explain it, like, further down on the page or tell about something and not tell what it means. You have to make sure you are going in the right direction with it so they understand what you are talking about through the whole paper.

Student Voice #2: Normally you just try to ramble off a whole bunch of big terms and get it done, and then you usually don't even understand what you are writing. I think it was because having to dumb some of the words down a little helped me to better understand what I was trying to talk about. Figuring out how to dumb it down, it helps you try to find out what it really is . . . just thinking about how they would understand things, and then if you think they could understand it, then there is a really good chance that you would understand it.

---

❖ Assessment of the writing piece can go through two layers. The first is the real audience that you have chosen—peers, younger students, parents, or the general public. The second is from you as the teacher. You need to provide some feedback to the students. However, we have encouraged teachers to do this during the second draft completed by the students. We have had teachers who have given the second draft back to the original audience participant to assess the piece as well, while others have assessed the piece without giving it back to the original audience participant.

Having established a framework for the writing experience, the students then need time and space to complete the exercise of producing their piece of writing. Many of the teachers we have worked with have assigned this individual piece of writing as a homework exercise. We believe that it is critical that each student produce his or her own piece of writing as this task is based on encouraging each individual student to construct his or her own understanding of how the concepts are linked together.

A critical element is to make sure that the audience for the piece of writing is real: Students need to understand that you as the teacher will be collecting their drafts and these will be given to the audience. We have consistently given the same scoring guide used by the teacher to audience participants and asked them to complete the guide to provide feedback to the student. The impact on older students when they receive feedback from younger students has been very informative. We have seen some very crestfallen students when younger students harshly criticize them because the science is not clearly explained, the writing is bad, or the whole thing does not make sense.

## Examples of the Summary-Writing Experience

Several summary-writing exercises that we have used follow. Remember that the intent of these pieces of writing was to complete the unit after the students had being involved in a number of SWH activities. We hope that these will help you set one up for an SWH experience in your own classroom.

1. Tenth-grade students who were studying biotechnology were asked to write a newspaper article about different uses of this technology when applied to local farming practices. The editor of the local newspaper was invited to speak to the students. He was involved in assessing the pieces, with the end result being he published two of the students' pieces.

2. Eleventh-grade chemistry students were asked to write a letter to seventh-grade students explaining stiochoimetry. The students were advised that they should use some form of analogy such as baking a cake to help their audience understand. The letters were collected and given to the seventh-grade students in the school. The seventh-grade students were unfamiliar with the topic and, thus, there was an emphasis placed on trying to have the eleventh-grade students clearly explain this difficult topic.

3. Seventh-grade students were asked to write a textbook explanation about classification for their peers. The student peers were students in the other seventh-grade classes and, thus, they were familiar with the big ideas addressed in the unit.

Each member was given a copy of the scoring guide to provide feedback to the authors of the written product. All the teachers attempted to provide opportunities for the students to redraft their original piece of writing, based on the feedback that they had received. Figure 8.3 contains two samples of scoring guides. The first is a generic form and the second is from a classroom that was studying a unit on chemical reactions.

The examples in Figures 8.4 show students using a variety of writing types. As you look at the samples, look for the big ideas and for comprehension of the science.

> **HAVE A GO!**
> **ASSESSING STUDENT WRITING**
>
> What is it that you value in the writing of your students? Go to Appendix L to explore writing from your student as well as illuminate what your expectations are for high-quality science writing.

# Revisiting the Big Idea

The writing that the students do in completing the SWH report is focused on building argument as well as giving each student the opportunity to describe his or her understanding of the big ideas explored through the SWH experience. The students are trying to frame a scientific argument through writing by answering the questions on the various sections of Questions, Procedure, Observations, Claims, Evidence, Reading, and Reflection. The purpose of the writing is for the students to link these various components together.

**Figure 8.3.** *Scoring guides*

## Generic Scoring Guide

| | More effort needed | Making progress | Satisfactory effort | Good work |
|---|---|---|---|---|
| Big ideas clearly indicated | | | | |
| Big ideas clearly explained | | | | |
| Writing is appropriate for audience | | | | |
| Writing matches the format asked for | | | | |
| Diagrams, graphs, etc. help explain the big ideas | | | | |

**Figure 8.3.** *(Continued)*

## Grading Guide for Chemistry Cartoons

| Content | 0 | 1 | 2 | 3 | Total | Score |
|---|---|---|---|---|---|---|
| Topic description/ definition | Absent | Inaccurate | Adequate | Accurate and Complete | 3 | |
| Chem. concepts I, reactions need energy | Absent | Inaccurate | Adequate | X | 2 | |
| Chem. concept 2, conservation of mass | Absent | Included | Relevant | X | 2 | |
| Chem. concept 3, reactions are electron transactions | Absent | Incomplete or Inaccurate | Adequate | X | 2 | |
| Science of the chemistry is accurate | Absent | Inaccurate | Incomplete | Complete | 3 | |
| Example used | Absent | Included | Relevant | X | 2 | |

# From the Students

These writing assignments represent story writing, poetry, and pictorial writing. In each case, the student was forced to negotiate not only the science but also the language. Translation from the science language into a language that was appropriate for the writing forces the learner to struggle with the ideas and make connections in their head to ideas outside the science framework they built in the SWH approach.

**Figure 8.4.**  *Examples of student summary-writing experiences*

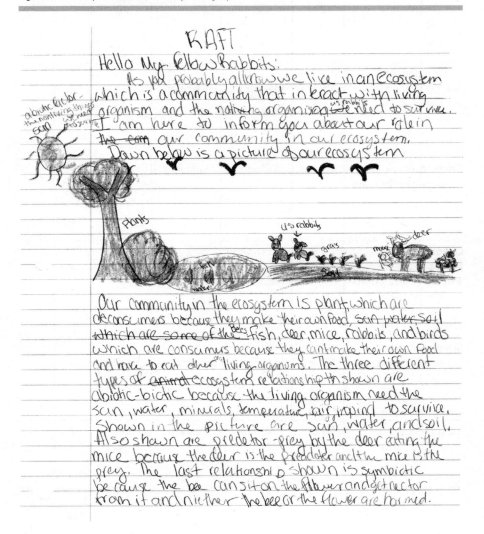

**Figure 8.4.** *(Continued)*

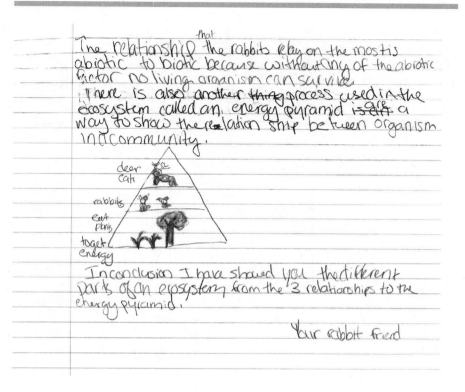

The relationship <sup>that</sup> the rabbits rely on the most is abiotic to biotic because without any of the abiotic factor no living organism can survive. There is also another ~~thing~~ process used in the ecosystem called an energy pyramid is a a way to show the relation ship between organism in community.

In conclusion I have showed you the different parts of an ecosystem from the 3 relationships to the energy pyramid.

Your rabbit friend

*continues on next page*

**Figure 8.4.** *(Continued)*

Chlorophyl–gives plants their green color

Every living thing is made of cells (cell the

Leaf cells–make a leaf on a plant (make the food for

Little organelles–help the cell function

Skin cells–make a protective layer of skin

# Examining Our Own Practice

W e began this book by posing a question to begin our investigation to-gether: How do I teach science in the service of learning . . . where the learning for each of my students is maximized, providing opportunities to not only grow in their science understanding but also to include opportunities to grow as readers, writers, and mathematicians? In the following pages, we will chal-lenge you to examine your own teaching and to engage in an active investigation of your teaching practices and how they support student learning. A matrix is provided to guide your inquiries (Chapter 9) as well as a frequently asked questions section (Chapter 10) addressing some of the very questions that may have you perplexed. In addition, this final chapter provides an overview of the research conducted on the SWH approach and implications for its use in classrooms.

**Figure III.1.** *Teacher working with students in an SWH classroom*

# Measuring Your Progress

Having read the previous chapters and having begun to explore what the strategies look like in the classroom, the question is now, how well are you implementing the suggestions that we have put forward? In this chapter, we will provide you with a performance matrix, which you can use as a tool to examine where you are in the process. This performance matrix is the same one that we use with all of our research into the use of the Science Writing Heuristic and thus represents much work into teacher efforts toward using the strategies.

Before we talk about what components and strategies that as teachers we need to concentrate on for changing to use the SWH approach in our own classrooms, we must talk about the time it takes. All the teachers we have worked with have found that change is slow, that is, it is not instantaneous or linear—it takes time to adjust to new strategies. Change is not instant; there is no sudden movement away from one style of teaching to another, and some days just go better than others. The process is truly an example of the "two steps forward, one step back" cliché. We have to change some of our thinking, change how that thinking transfers into the classroom, and then respond to the changes in the classroom that result. To make matters worse, as you start out with simple changes, the complexity of all the changes meshed together makes you realize how difficult the whole process is. However, the end results are certainly worth going through the whole change process, so fight the urge to say that this process isn't worth all the effort. Despite the difficulties and effort, moving toward a practicing level is quite energizing both personally and professionally.

Before moving into the components and practices involved, we would like to remind everyone that management is a critical component of the SWH approach and any inquiry approach. While we are promoting student-centered learning strategies, this does not mean that the teacher does not have to deal with management. As discussed previously, as teachers we need to manage behavior, materials, and the curriculum. All the components and practices we talk about next require that as teachers you maintain good management strategies. Remember, the setting up of a nonthreatening learning environment where all students are able to participate requires that good and meaningful management strategies are in place. "Student-centered" does not mean a lack of effort on our part as teachers; rather it will take more effort on our part. *But the rewards are worth it.*

## A Tool to Assist in Examining Your Development

The matrix was designed by looking over observations with teachers and attempting to find a way to describe what we were seeing happen in successful classrooms. We began with what we called a "profile of implementation" because our goal was to demonstrate the developmental nature of this learning process—a process that is ongoing and dynamic. We wanted the profiles to reflect this. However, the narrative lists were a bit hard to manage so we consulted the work of Douglas Llewellyn (2001) and appreciated the table format of his rubrics for becoming an inquiry-based teacher. We moved to this tabular format but chose to specifically focus on four essential traits that we have seen emerge in successful implementation of the SWH approach.

In trying to determine how we can best help teachers improve their practices, we developed a matrix that has four major component areas that we use for classroom observations and four categories of success. These categories are:

❖ Beginning. This level is where the teacher is beginning to investigate the strategies. While they are beginning they tend to be keeping the major focus on themselves as teachers, rather than on the students.

❖ Approaching. This level is where the teacher is beginning to build the components and is attempting to use them on a more consistent basis; the major focus is the student occasionally.

❖ Understanding. This level is where the teacher is beginning to move away from their previous teacher-centered practices and be more consistent in implementing the required components. The focus has shifted to the student more often than the teacher.

❖ Practicing. This level is where the teacher is consistently using student-centered practices and the focus is primarily on the student.

As we outline in the following matrix, remember that as teachers we are constantly moving between components of a lesson. We have to adapt and change actions as the lesson unfolds, and thus it is nearly impossible to identify and "score" every component of a lesson. However, what we have attempted to do is to provide a guideline to where you as teacher could be in terms of your practice. It is extremely difficult for us to judge ourselves—some of us are too hard on ourselves; others of us tend to overestimate our levels of achievement. The intent of the matrix is to help you begin to see some strengths and weaknesses and the areas that require improvement.

# Major Components

In looking at how to help teachers and determining the focal areas needed to ensure good implementation of the SWH strategies, we have used four major components that have implication for teacher practice. These are:

Dialogical Interactions

Focus of Learning

Connections

Science Argument

Each of these major components has a particular focus that when added together helps teachers be successful. Remember, all the components are interconnected—while we have broken them down into some separate areas, these are distinctly connected. Building strength in one area will help with others, thus there is a need to build all the areas. However, the reverse is not true—concentrating on only one area will not give you strength in the others. Another critical point to remember as you begin the process is that we can concentrate on one or two areas to begin with and the whole process may appear to be simple. However, the more we try the strategies and examine the process, the more complex it becomes. That is not a problem; we just have to remember that it takes time and we have to work at it. Next we explain each of these components.

## Dialogical Interaction

An absolutely crucial element of the SWH approach is the importance that is placed on negotiation of meaning. Students need to have opportunities to talk with each other in small groups, with their peers as a whole group, and with the teacher. Traditional teaching has centered on the teacher being in charge of the talk: They have structured the types of discussions allowed with emphasis on the teacher being in charge of what is discussed and what knowledge is allowed. This has resulted in most questioning being the *Initiate Respond Evaluate* pattern (Cazden, 2001) with the teacher being at the center, controlling the whole process. Shifting to student-centered learning strategies means that this orientation changes—students construct their own knowledge and, thus, there is a need for us as teachers to challenge this knowledge. This strategy requires us to engage the students' knowledge in a public forum, using questions that challenge and extend understanding. However, most important, we need to listen to students. *Dialogue is not about a monologue from the teacher.* It requires us to *both talk and listen.* Dialogue is about continuing a conversation and requires us to interact with the knowledge put forward by others so that the conversation continues to build. For us as teachers, this is often the toughest challenge for us: to remove ourselves from the center of the conversation. It takes practice. We have provided some examples to explore some of the categories of implementation look like in practice:

*Beginning:* Teachers who are in this category are generally doing two things. The first is that all discussion is coming through the teacher. There are very few or almost no opportunities for students to initiate a dialogue, as the teacher is concerned about making sure he or she is in control of the knowledge being dealt with in the classroom setting. Second, the teachers generally do not ask probing questions, or if they do they are seeking a single answer. In this stage we find teachers begin to ask more opened-ended questions. However, they step back from allowing the student voice to be part of the process.

*Approaching:* Teachers in this category are beginning to ask open-ended questions and try to not evaluate the student response, but fail to follow up with probing questions to explore student thinking. In part, they are beginning to change their questioning strategies and need time to get used to the change. Teachers in this category also begin to attempt to have student-to-student discussion in class, rather than always being the center of attention. However, this is generally not the focus of the talk in the classroom.

*Understanding:* Teachers in this category are beginning to increase the frequency of student-to-student dialogue in the classroom. Students are starting to be asked to explain and challenge each other's responses rather than the teacher passing judgment. Teachers are using a broad array of questions that begin to probe student understandings. Teachers are beginning to place emphasis on having a conversation with their students with the intention of building understanding rather than memorizing the vocabulary of the topic.

*Practicing:* Teachers in this category are constantly using teacher-student dialogue and student-to-student dialogue to challenge ideas, claims, and evidence. A broad array of questions is used with the focus on approaching students' understandings of the topic. While being aware of individual needs, the teacher has an expectation of involvement for all students, with all being required to be part of the dialogue. Student responses are constantly challenged, probed, and extended.

**Figure 9.1.**  *Dialogical interaction aspect of the matrix*

| | Level 1 Beginning | Level 2 Approaching | Level 3 Understanding | Level 4 Practicing |
|---|---|---|---|---|
| Dialogical Interactions | • All discussion coming through the teacher; no or few opportunities for students to initiate a dialogue<br>• Teacher seeks single correct answer, no probing questions<br>• Teacher uses IRE pattern (Initiates, Responds, Evaluates) of questioning | • Teacher attempts student-to-student discussion; provides some opportunities for students to initiate a dialogue<br>• Teacher begins to ask open-ended questions<br>• Teacher begins to use non-evaluative questioning | • Teacher increasing frequency of student-to-student dialogue<br>• Teacher asks many layers of questions (i.e., Bloom's Taxonomy) to begin probing student understanding<br>• Teacher asks students to explain and challenge each other's responses rather than pass judgment<br>• Teachers beginning to place emphasis on having a conversation with the intention of building student understanding | • Teacher constantly using teacher-student dialogue and student-to-student dialogue to challenge ideas, claims, and evidence<br>• Teacher asks many layers of questions (i.e., Bloom's Taxonomy) to build student understanding<br>• Teacher constantly challenges, probes, and extends student responses<br>• Teacher has expectation of all students being involved in the dialogue while being aware of individual needs |

## Focus of Learning

In the early chapters of this book, we have focused on who controls learning and how to adopt student-centered strategies. This is absolutely critical in terms of promoting strategies that enable students to become engaged in learning science and expanding their language use. This approach requires teachers to change their focus of planning. If learning is about the construction of conceptual frameworks, then teaching has to be oriented toward the "big ideas" or concepts of the topic. This focus on the big idea then needs to be translated into classroom practice. For us the question becomes how do we continue to focus on helping students engage with the big ideas of the topic? Do we as teachers have a list of content that drives our planning or do we have a number of big ideas that frame our planning? Is our planning loose enough to deal with unexpected events in class? One of the major problems teachers have is to maintain a focus that encourages students to wrestle with their understandings of the concepts that underpin the topic. When in small groups students need to have discussions that not only deal with the event/question engaged with but also question how all this fits with the big idea of the topic. The planning needs to build in opportunities for small-group discussions, flexibility to move with different student questions/ideas/suggestions about concepts that are not part of the plan, and ability to move between individual, small-group, and whole-class settings. The difference between a teacher-centered and student-centered classroom is that the focus of learning is not on what the teacher knows and gives to the students, but rather how the teacher constantly strives to engage the students' knowledge and uses this knowledge as the platform for instruction.

*Beginning:* Teachers in this category tend to plan only for whole-class instruction with the emphasis being on ensuring that they are able to cover the content of the topic. The focus of the SWH is to complete the student template as though it were a worksheet. Students are not provided time to share knowledge and tend to play "guess what is in the teacher's head" games when answering questions.

*Approaching:* In this category, teachers begin to build into their plans some opportunities for students to work in small groups. On some occasions unexpected results from students are used to add to the lesson, but the emphasis is still on making sure teacher knowledge is the guiding frame of the lesson. The SWH process is moving away from being simply a worksheet. There is some emphasis on ensuring there are connections between claims and evidence and gathering different viewpoints.

*Understanding:* Teachers in this category regularly plan on using small-group work as a critical component of the lesson, with student knowledge being used within the lesson. There is more comfort with the flexible nature of the SWH process. However, there is still some tension between teacher-centered and student-centered components of knowledge that are dealt with in class. Students are expected to be able to engage in discussions and debates about the topic in framing the arguments that are derived from the inquiry process. Teachers are becoming more comfortable with the degree of flexibility required of the approach.

*Practicing:* Teachers in this category continually and effectively plan for opportunities for students to be involved in small-group and whole-class work. Teachers are flexible and prepared to move in unanticipated directions. They constantly seek student input and challenge ideas that are brought forward. In this category teachers are comfortable with the whole SWH approach and are effectively linking the components of Question, Claims, Evidence, and Reflection together.

## Connections

The emphasis of the SWH approach is on the connections that it makes to a range of different areas. Three critical areas of connection are the embedded language practices, the big ideas of the topic, and assessment. The use of language in terms of reading, talking, and writing is absolutely critical in the SWH approach, and thus, it is important for teachers to constantly make connections to the language components. Examples of this include the public debates about each group's claim and evidence to emphasize the scientific argumentation process; the writing up of the claims and evidence to ensure that students are making reasoned statements linking these together; the use of different reading sources for determining the validity of claims; and the summary-writing exercise to connect the activities together conceptually. The second area is the connection to the big idea(s) of the unit. As discussed in the early chapters, learning is about the construction of conceptual understanding and the development of conceptual frameworks. To assist this we believe that learning must be focused on the conceptual framework, and thus, teachers need to constantly make connections to this organizing frame of the topic, that is, the big ideas. The third area is that of assessment. As teachers we need to move away from multiple-choice questions, fill-in-the-blanks, match-the-words, and short-answer questions. If we are going to involve students in activities that purposefully challenge their ideas, require them to think critically, and reason about problems and solutions to problems, then we need to assess them in a manner that reflects this approach. Thus we need to use conceptual questions that require students to connect knowledge, explain their understanding, and justify their arguments. These questions need to be about the conceptual framework of the topic, rather than focusing solely on the content points of the topic. Questions need to be extended-response-type questions that require and allow students opportunities to fully answer the questions.

**Figure 9.2.** *Focus of learning aspect of the matrix*

| | Level 1 Beginning | Level 2 Approaching | Level 3 Understanding | Level 4 Practicing |
|---|---|---|---|---|
| Focus of Learning | • Teacher uses only whole-class grouping for instruction <br> • Focus of SWH is on completion of template <br> • Teacher-centered, teacher-controlled <br> • Displays little confidence in SWH process <br> • No student sharing of knowledge | • Teacher uses whole-class grouping with occasional small groups for instruction <br> • SWH process evident in some connections made between claims and evidence, and gathering different viewpoints <br> • Teacher-centered, but occasionally student-centered <br> • Developing confidence in SWH <br> • Some student sharing, but emphasis on teacher knowledge | • Teacher regularly uses a variety of grouping strategies for instruction <br> • SWH process evident in stronger connections between claims and evidence, and gathering of different viewpoints <br> • A balance of teacher- and student-centered activities <br> • Shows confidence in flexibility of SWH approach <br> • Students expected to engage in discussions and debates about the topic in framing arguments | • Teacher thoughtfully plans for a variety of appropriate grouping strategies for instruction <br> • SWH process evident in strong connections between claims and evidence, gathering of different viewpoints, and reflections on understanding <br> • Obvious confidence in SWH approach <br> • Students sharing with argumentation with few prompts needed |

*Beginning:* Teachers in this category do not make connections to the big ideas of the topic; instead there is only fleeting references to these. Little emphasis is placed on the use of language-based strategies such as diversifying the types of writing used in the classroom, little opportunities for student talk to promote understanding, and reliance on a single information source. Assessment does not reflect the critical thinking and reasoning demands of the approach and is focused on recall of information.

*Approaching:* Teachers in this category begin to focus on the big ideas of the topic but tend to do so in a mechanical fashion, that is, they highlight the big ideas but do not use these for building the topic. There is some emphasis on determining student ideas; however, while the teachers seek out these ideas, there is no attempt to build on them. Teachers are beginning to embed some language practices and begin to place emphasis on student participation in these activities. Assessment is beginning to focus on challenging students' thinking, while still using mostly memory-recall items.

*Understanding:* Teachers in this category connect science to everyday life and build on student knowledge. There is an emphasis on determining student knowledge and building teaching plans based on this knowledge. The big ideas are becoming central to the teaching plan and to the assessment completed by the students. The concept of assessment is better balanced between recall-type questions and extended-response questions. Instruction is flexible and uses opportunities for language-based activities to build knowledge.

*Practicing:* Teachers in this category are consistently using opportunities to connect science with everyday life. They consistently frame their teaching around the big ideas of the topic and promote student learning around these big ideas. Students are constantly required to engage in language practices that promote understanding, for example, diversified writing is undertaken, public debate promotes the function of talk in learning, and multiple sources of information are used to promote reading of a broad range of informational text. Assessment practices are clearly aligned to the curriculum in using recall and extended-response questions.

## Science Argument

The fundamental essence of the SWH approach is the promotion of scientific argumentation. The structure scaffolds and promotes the scientific argument framework of question, claims, evidence, and reflection. Thus the final focus area is on this critical component. The elements that are essential are opportunities for students to pose questions, to construct a concise statement—a claim—as a result of their inquiry, to provide reasoned evidence for their claims, and to ensure that they determine how their claims and evidence match up to what is currently known about the topic

**Figure 9.3.**  *Connections aspect of the matrix*

| | Level 1 Beginning | Level 2 Approaching | Level 3 Understanding | Level 4 Practicing |
|---|---|---|---|---|
| Connections | • Teacher does not make connections to the big ideas of the topic<br>• Science activities do not promote big ideas of the topic<br>• Little emphasis on the use of literacy strategies to promote understanding<br>• Reliance on textbook as single resource<br>• Teacher does not build on or activate students' initial understanding<br>• Assessment does not align with intended and taught curriculum | • Teacher connection to the big ideas of the topic is mechanical<br>• Science activities promote big ideas of the topic in a vague way<br>• Some emphasis on the use of literacy strategies to promote understanding<br>• Beginning use of other resources besides textbook<br>• Teacher moves toward revealing students' initial understanding but fails to use information to make instructional decisions<br>• Assessments may align to curriculum but are recall focused | • Teacher connection to the big ideas of the topic emphasized<br>• Science activities connected to the big ideas of the topic<br>• Literacy activities used, both planned and unplanned, to promote understanding<br>• Various resources, both print and nonprint, used<br>• Teacher works to reveal students' initial understanding and make instructional decisions based on the information<br>• Assessments align to curriculum with a beginning balance of recall and extended-response-type questions | • Teacher consistently frames teaching around big ideas of the topic<br>• Science activities connected to the big ideas of the topic and extend students' learning<br>• Literacy activities, both planned and unplanned, promote and extend understanding<br>• Consistent use of various resources, both print and nonprint<br>• Teacher effectively reveals students' initial understanding and makes instructional decisions based on the information<br>• Assessments aligned to curriculum with a balance of recall and extended-response-type questions |

(reflection). The investigations and argument structures are centered on the big ideas of the topic, and thus, we believe it is important that the teachers insist that the arguments being constructed by the students are centered on and matched to the big ideas framing the unit study.

*Beginning:* Teachers in this category are reluctant to promote student input into the questions for inquiry. Instead they pose the question to be investigated and provide the answers that students are expected to have come up with for the unit. There is also a lack of emphasis on student input into the discussion of the data, with little of no attempt made to use the terminology of claims and evidence. As a result there is very limited use of the scientific argument pattern of Question, Claims, Evidence, and Reflection. Thus, little attempt is made to build argument connected to the big ideas of the topic.

*Approaching:* Teachers in this category are beginning to build in opportunities, though these are limited, for students to pose some questions for the inquiry. The idea of claims and evidence is starting to appear in the teacher dialogue, with some attempt to ensure that science argument structure is provided to the students. Connections to the big ideas of the topic are made; however, the teacher is providing limited opportunities for the students to debate their ideas in relation to the big ideas.

*Understanding:* Teachers in this category provide opportunities for students to pose questions and revise them where needed. Students are required to link claims and evidence, that is, students are not allowed to make a claim without providing some form of evidence. The teacher does not consistently scaffold the scientific argument process of Question, Claims, Evidence, and Reflection. The big idea of the topic is a central focus of the inquiry, and students are provided some opportunities to debate their ideas in relation to the topic.

*Practicing:* Teachers in this category provide opportunities for students to pose questions and revise them where needed. Students are consistently required to link claims and evidence and to use scientific argument where links between Question, Claims, Evidence, and Reflection are made. Connections to the big idea of the unit are consistently made and students are required to be involved in debate about these ideas.

# How to Use the Matrix

Having outlined the components and categories for implementation, we need to discuss how to use the matrix. A critical point to remember is that it is difficult for us as individuals to examine our teaching practices by ourselves by just thinking back

**Figure 9.4.** *Science argument aspect of the matrix*

| | Level 1 Beginning | Level 2 Approaching | Level 3 Understanding | Level 4 Practicing |
|---|---|---|---|---|
| Science Argument (Questions, Claims, and Evidence) | • Teacher very reluctant to promote student input into the questions for inquiry<br>• Teacher generates the answer to the problem solving<br>• Very limited use of terminology of claims and evidence<br>• Very limited use of scientific argumentation pattern<br>• Little attempt to build argument connected to the big ideas of the topic | • Teacher begins to build limited opportunities for students to pose some questions for revise them the inquiry<br>• Idea of claims and evidence starting to appear in teacher dialogue<br>• Some attempt to ensure science argument structure provided to students<br>• Teacher provides limited opportunities for students to build argument connected to the big ideas of the topic | • Teacher provides opportunities for students to pose questions and some attempt to where needed<br>• Teacher requires students to link claims and evidence<br>• Some scaffolding of instruction provided for the scientific argument process<br>• Big ideas of the topic are the central focus of the inquiry and students are provided some opportunities to debate their ideas | • Teacher provides opportunities for students to pose questions and revise them where needed<br>• Teacher consistently requires students to link claims and evidence<br>• Teacher consistently requires students to use scientific argument where links between question, claims, evidence, and reflection are made<br>• Connections to the big ideas of the unit are consistently made and students are required to be involved in debates about these ideas |

through the lesson we have just taught. There is a need for us to make a plan to have opportunities to reflect back on what actually occurred in the lesson. This can be done a number of different ways:

Have a colleague sit in your room and make notes. We encourage you to focus on a particular component rather than on all the different components.

Videotape the lesson. This may be a little time-consuming, but it is a good way for you to see exactly what you were doing.

Involve your students in helping you stay on task for a particular component of questioning, promoting dialogue, or making claims and evidence, for example. We have had success when implementing these types of components by explaining to the students that we have been involved in doing a research project to become a better teacher to help them learn.

Whatever strategies you use to examine your teaching, there is a need to understand the amount of time needed. Improvement in what we do requires practice and reflection.

While the matrix has been presented as a number of categories and components, we encourage you to focus on one component in particular as a means to improve all the components. The components are interconnected and should be seen as such. However, to change or improve all the components at one time is a difficult task. Thus, we suggest some of the following possible strategies:

Plan to use the basic structure of the SWH, that is, plan to make sure the concepts of Question, Claims, Evidence, and Reflection are built into your lesson.

Choose one of the components—for example, dialogical interaction—and define what you think are your strengths and weaknesses with this component.

Prepare a few cues that you could use to practice the component. For example, instead of confirming a student's answer, ask another student; ask students for clarification of their answers; move away from "guess what is in my head" games.

Plan a process that allows for monitoring of your component.

Find a colleague who you can work with to review the analysis of the lesson.

Plan for the next practice session—changing components is a tough task and requires practice.

As you get better at one component begin to examine how this component meshes with another of the components in the matrix.

We cannot stress enough that we as teachers need to remove ourselves from the center of the action. The greatest turning point for teachers that we have found is when they stop talking, get out of the way, and let the students do the thinking. The components outlined are about making student-centered learning environments the focus of our teaching.

Do not be discouraged when everything does not go as planned or if things quickly become too complicated. Raise the bar on your level of expectation for yourself and your students and you will find that change will take place in your classroom.

# Examples of Implementation

Next we have tried to provide two case studies of implementation that we hope will help you understand some of the challenges that we as teachers face in using these approaches. We would like to reiterate that there is no single pathway to success—we all have different ways that we do things. However, we do know that constantly striving to challenge students' thinking and requiring science argument is critical in promoting understanding of the science concepts. The case studies described next are constructed from a number of different studies that we have been involved with and do not reflect any one teacher.

## Case study 1

Bill is an experienced middle/secondary-school science teacher who has been using the SWH for two years. Bill has been using the student template as the report format for his students. The students are required to complete all sections of the template, and his marking scheme has equal points allocated for each section of the template. He is still struggling with his questioning components; at times he begins to pass student answers back to the group but too often steps back and seeks to play "guess what is in my head" games. He appears to lack confidence in students' abilities to think deeply and thus does not relax enough to give them opportunities to demonstrate that they can. This creates a catch-22 situation: Because he does not completely trust the students to address all the conceptual knowledge, he places emphasis on ensuring that he covers all the content knowledge. He struggles with balancing the coverage of content knowledge with the big ideas of the topic, thus he finds it difficult to focus learning on the big ideas of the topic. When he begins to let students have some space in terms of discussion of the ideas from the inquiry activities, he gets excited by what they are saying but struggles to move forward in using the students' ideas. In terms of planning for these activities he has not done enough forward planning in relation to constructing a concept map of the topic and thus is very concerned when students take the conversation away from his direction for the unit. We would say that *Bill is in the beginning stage but beginning to move toward the approaching stage*.

## Case study 2

Judy is an experienced secondary-school biology teacher who has been using the SWH strategies for three years. During this time she has continued to improve her components and has worked hard to be more student-centered in her use of the SWH approach. Her questioning of students is consistently focused on trying to explore students' understandings, where she ensures that students are constantly challenged when providing answers. Students are challenged to provide supporting evidence when making a claim both when talking about their activities and when writing up their SWH reports. At the completion of activities each small group is required to place their claims and evidence on the board. They are expected to explain their reasoning for their claim, and the class as a whole explores consensus for a whole-class-constructed claim. Judy struggles at times to link the science activities with some of the language activities that could strengthen student understanding. While she requires her students to use diversified types of writing to summarize the chapter, she does not consistently give students enough planning time. She is beginning to make better use of her concept map planning for the unit, in that she is now much more comfortable in allowing students to move along pathways that are not always productive in building knowledge. Having constructed the concept map she is now confident in being able to redirect students through her questioning strategies. We would say *that Judy is in the understanding phase moving into the practicing stage*.

## Revisiting the Big Idea

Remember, in trying to construct your own rating be realistic and fair to yourself. Change takes time and you need to keep practicing and view your own teaching practice. We began this book with a challenge to you—to become an active investigator of your own practice and to teach in the service of learning. To meet this challenge, you have to be willing to take a close look at your own practices and how they support (or hinder) your students and the learning opportunities that are made available to them. The matrix presented in this chapter is one way to get started.

# CHAPTER 10

# Frequently Asked Questions and Benefits of the SWH Approach

In this chapter we present some frequently asked questions for the reader. These questions were generated and answered by our consulting group of teachers. These teachers have used the SWH approach and were asked to put together some questions that they had wanted to know about when they started implementing the SWH in their own classrooms. While there are many possible questions, we kept the total to ten. Thus, they are more general in nature but we believe that they do answer some of the initial concerns of teachers.

We wanted to present to the reader some results that we have gathered in our research into using the SWH approach. We have been fortunate to work with a number of schools and their teachers, and have been able to explore what we believe are some critical questions about the benefits and difficulties that arise when using the SWH approach. While we present some general benefits, a list of publications is provided of the research articles and conference presentations that we have been involved with for further reading and investigation.

## Frequently Asked Questions

As we described earlier, the intent of this section is to provide the reader with some questions and answers from teachers who have used the SWH for a number of years. Thus the questions and answers are based on real experience and not in the imagination of the authors.

## How is SWH different from what you are already doing in your science classroom?

SWH puts the ownership for learning back in the hands of the student. To do well requires that you step back and stop thinking that as the teacher you can control what students learn. SWH also is a process that encourages students to negotiate their own learning and so now you get to find out what they "really" understand rather than what they want to give back to you.

I used to think that I was doing great with inquiry-type teaching, but I was not able to get the type of discussions that I can now generate with students. The student SWH template allows me to have a structure that promotes the student discussions about Questions, Claims, and Evidence that I did not have before. It is a change in mind-set. Once I realized that the students are in control of their own learning and I could not force them to learn what I thought was important, it began to click. It is about empowering students by guiding them through meaningful discussions— that develops true scientific thinkers. It takes time. It takes meaningful feedback from both students and other observers. Once you get the idea, students will not want you to go back to your "old" ways of cramming the curriculum down their throat.

## How do you get started with an SWH unit?

Look at your current plan for a unit and decide what the "big idea(s)" are. This sounds easy, but it was the hardest to deal with at the beginning. I had to change from looking at what I needed to cover to what were the one or two things I wanted students to have when they left my classroom. The other part about getting started was to realize that I did not have to start from scratch. I was able to use questions like, "What do you do that already that will tie in with the big ideas?" Can you modify existing activities so that they could involve an inquiry approach? What activities could you plan that will allow the students to inquire? What do you have to get ready to guide my planning? I would say that I am as prepared as I always am; I just have to go about it differently.

## What are your priorities as a teacher of SWH?

There is no easy answer to this question because there are a number of things that I believe are priorities. These include that I need to know the big ideas, I need to create concept maps for those big ideas, and I need to have a comfort with the concepts/ content of material I am teaching. I think it would be hard to teach a unit of science using the SWH approach for the first time in a topic area that I was very uncomfortable with. In terms of the actual classroom my top priority is to get better at questioning. I need to keep quiet and get the kids to talk more. I know that I spend too much time trying to control the conversation rather than letting the kids run with the discussion. I need to challenge the kids more—I do not make them justify claims with evidence as much as I should. This is going to take some time.

## What strategies are used in a typical unit?

The unit usually begins with a concept map. It is critical to find out what your students actually know. This makes sense; however, we as teachers usually don't take interest in this. We think we know what they should learn and don't give the students a voice in the matter. Once you find out what they know about a given topic, it is critical that this information is made public. Posting the ideas on poster paper and displaying them in the room gives the students a constant reminder of what they already know. From here, the teacher begins designing a big idea. What is it that is most important? What can they constantly come back and connect to their new learning. For example, when doing a unit on "Forces," my big idea was, "A force is a push or pull." Then, I began to design SWH labs that could be connected to this big idea.

## Does the SWH process slow you down in covering the curriculum?

It may. I know that I have only a certain amount of time for each topic so I have to fit the SWH approach to the time available. However, I find that the units often seem to connect to each other better because of using the SWH approach. The connections students make with the big ideas are carried over to other units. I find that I am less conscious of trying to cover content and focus much more on the concepts that I need to deal with. I did find that when I started to use the SWH approach it did take me a little longer to cover the first couple of units. The more I used the SWH, the more comfortable I became in dealing with the curriculum. I do admit that sometimes due to time I will have to wrap up a unit earlier than planned.

## How do you manage the grading of the writing?

If you have a lot of students taking a class and each of them are writing an SWH and writing answers for concept questions on tests, the reading and grading of papers may seem to be overwhelming at first. I have eliminated some types of homework so that students can spend time on their writing, and this reduces the amount of marking. I have also used students to help with some of the marking—they can be trained to help in evaluation, particularly with first-draft efforts. It really helps if you have a scoring device ready to weight the areas of the SWH and concept questions. Questions I have used to help me shape the scoring device are: How many points should be given to areas of the SWH or questions? What is the critical idea that I think is important? I have always given the scoring device for the SWH to the students at the start of using the approach.

## What are the benefits of the SWH approach?

The change in the classroom is the big gain. I found the change to be positive for both the students and myself. Making my classroom more student-centered has meant that I have found that students are doing more thinking, connecting, and learning. I find that I am challenging the students to do more on their own and leading them in discussion of the key concepts or big ideas. They are beginning to be much more careful when making claims about the inquiry and now are providing evidence to support what they are claiming. This means that they are more prepared to think through the ideas that they talk about than they were previously. The students are getting more benefit from reading and writing, and hopefully it will show up on the ways the school district is measured.

## Do all students accept the SWH approach?

This is an interesting question because I have found that students who do well and are accustomed to the more traditional approaches of teaching may balk at first because they already learn well. They want to be told and it bothers them that the answers to questions are not going to be given to them. They are the students who want the assignment, the immediate feedback, and the answer. They are the ones that are good at "playing" school. All of a sudden, the rules of the game have changed and they don't like it. When they realize the benefits and the fact that they are challenged, most will eventually appreciate the inquiry approach. Conversely, I have found that students who are generally quiet and do not participate are becoming much more involved and more vocal in class. These students are normally meek and lack confidence; however, they tend to benefit the quickest from this paradigm shift in the classroom. They enjoy having a voice that they know will not be criticized.

## What concerns do you have about SWH?

For me time is one of my major concerns. It takes time to get through the first couple of units because I had to adjust to things like allowing for student input and changing my questioning strategies. Because the planning is a little different this also takes time to adjust to. Having to change from covering the content to focusing on big ideas meant that I had to spend time trying to work out the big ideas and making sure the activities would line up with these big ideas. The other major concern I have is the opportunity to see someone teach using the SWH or to talk with someone who is using it at the same time that I am. I am often wondering if I am doing the "right" thing. However, I must say that these concerns do not stop me using the SWH—the students do really benefit.

## Can I change the order of the questions on the student template?

One of the real struggles that I had at the beginning was thinking that every time I used the SWH I had to make sure that every question was answered in the order it was laid out. It did help provide the framework to help me get the students going, but over a period of time I began to realize that it was okay to change some of the order of questions. For example, sometimes students would start their inquiry and have a second question arise before they had made a claim. Initially, I would not let them pursue the second question before doing Claims, Evidence, Reading, and Reflection sections. However, I now make a decision that if the second question is related, then I will get them to make their claims and evidence based on both questions. This took me some time to get comfortable with this approach.

## How long before you were comfortable with the SWH process?

I am not sure there is a comfort zone in SWH. I am not sure there should be. I have been doing this for two years and I believe I am still scratching the surface. I will say that to fully implement the SWH process takes longer than two years. I do not know yet what the magic number is, and I am not certain that I will ever have that answer. The SWH program should continue to strengthen, and each school year brings a dimension to SWH that I had not fully developed the previous year.

## Benefits of the SWH Approach

We have been involved in researching the implementation of the SWH approach for the last eight years. During this time we have students in preschool classrooms through to freshman chemistry students at a university using this approach. A number of clear benefits have been achieved using this approach. However, the benefits depend on the quality of the implementation. We cannot stress this enough. The SWH approach is a combination of teacher quality and embedded-language-based science-inquiry experiences. One by itself will not lead to the same result as the combination. Embedded-language practices, scientific argumentation, or teacher implementation alone will not give the same benefits as integrating all of these together.

In discussing the benefits, we point out that the results indicated have all been shown to be statistically significant, and papers reporting these are listed at the end of this chapter. Our studies have attempted to measure the difference between high- and low-quality implementation of the SWH approach to determine what students think about using the strategies and how one particular district has responded to its teachers using the approach. The benefits include:

1. *Closing the achievement gap.* The SWH approach has been successful in closing the gap between low achievers and high achievers. This has occurred with students at the middle school, high school, and university level. The gap is not closed but is significantly reduced. High-achieving students' scores have remained the same while the low-achieving students' scores are increased. In some cases we have half the gap between the pretest and posttest measures. In other studies, the gap has been almost closed, while in one study with tenth-grade students we have the low-achieving students outperforming the high-achieving students.

2. *Closing the gender gap.* Much attention has been focused on the disparity between genders in relation to science teaching in school. We have shown that we have been able to close this gap when students are engaged with the SWH approach. Interestingly, the low-achieving males are successful using this approach, not just females.

3. *Performance on Iowa Test of Basic Skills.* In the school district that we have been working with for three consecutive years, their scores on the less-proficient level have fallen from the low 30 percent range to the high teens percent range. This takes into account a range of teacher implementation levels. These students have moved into the proficient range, with the percentage of students at above profi- cient remaining relatively constant.

4. *Benefits for students with Individual Educational Programs (IEP students).* The inter- esting benefits seen with this group of students is that while raw scores are lower than non-IEP students, their rate of improvement in science is greater than the non-IEP students with high-quality implementation. These students become more engaged and tend to improve their conceptual understandings in a richer way than when using more traditional approaches.

5. *Benefits for low socioeconomic status (SES) students.* As with the IEP students we have seen gains made by the SES students that close the gap between non-SES and SES students. In a study with grades four, five, and six, SES students with high levels of implementation outperformed the non-SES students.

While these results point to the benefits gained in terms of statistical data, we have conducted interviews with students over a number of years. From these interviews we can also note a number of clear benefits that students believe arise from being involved with the SWH approach. These include:

1. *A greater control over the activity leads to more involvement in the activity.* Students consistently point to the ability to pose questions and have some control over the direction of the activity leading to a much greater sense of having some control of what they are able to do. This applies not only to the actual activity but also to their willingness to be involved in the discussion and debates.

2. *Students believe that they are learning when they use the SWH approach.* Students indicate that having to make claims and provide evidence and having to compare their answers with others has a very positive outcome for them in terms of their learning. They believe that as a consequence of the question structure they are involved with, they begin to understand the big ideas of the topic.

3. *Students believe that they are more confident in answering test questions.* When asked how confident they feel about answering test questions, the students have consistently told us that they feel more confident than when using traditional lab reports. Even though little time is spent on answering end-of-chapter questions, they feel that with the big ideas and discussions in class, they are confident about doing well on the test.

In summary, we remind the reader that we believe the SWH approach does have benefit for both teachers and students. However, these benefits will vary and may take time to materialize. We can say that the better we as teachers implement the SWH approach, the richer the benefits are for the students.

## Articles and Resources About the Research on the SWH Approach

*(Also, visit our website for a complete list of publications and presentations as well as links to a variety of papers and multimedia presentations.)*

Website Address: http://www.ci.hs.iastate.edu/scilit

Burke, Kathy, Jason Poock, Thomas Greenbowe, and Brian Hand. 2005. "Training Chemistry Teaching Assistants to Use the Science Writing Heuristic." *Journal of College Science Teaching* 35 (1): 36–41.

Greenbowe, Thomas J., and Brian Hand. 2005. "Introduction to the Science Writing Heuristic." In Norbert J. Pienta, Melanie M. Cooper, and Thomas J. Greenbowe, eds. *Chemists' Guide to Effective Teaching*. Upper Saddle River, NJ: Prentice Hall.

Hand, Brian, ed. 2008. *Science Inquiry, Argument, and Language: The Case for the Science Writing Heuristic (SWH)*. Rotterdam, the Netherlands: Sense Publishers.

Hand, Brian, Liesl Hohenshell, and Vaughn Prain. 2004. "Exploring Students' Responses to Conceptual Questions When Engaged with Planned Writing Experiences: A Study with Year 10 Science Students." *Journal of Research in Science Teaching* 41: 186–210.

Hand, Brian, Carolyn Wallace, and Eun-Mi Yang. 2004. "Using the Science Writing Heuristic to Enhance Learning Outcomes from Laboratory Activities in Seventh Grade Science: Quantitative and Qualitative Aspects." *International Journal of Science Education* 26: 131–49.

Hohenshell, Liesl, and Brian Hand. 2006. "Writing-to-Learn Strategies in Secondary School Cell Biology." *International Journal of Science Education* 28: 261–89.

Norton-Meier, Lori, Brian Hand, Lynn Hockenberry, and Kim Wise. 2008. *Questions, Claims, and Evidence: The Important Place of Argument in Children's Science Writing*. Portsmouth, NH: Heinemann.

Rudd, James A., Thomas J. Greenbowe, and Brian Hand. 2001. "Reshaping the General Chemistry Laboratory Report Using the Science Writing Heuristic." *Journal of College Science Teaching* 31: 230–34.

Rudd, James A., Thomas J. Greenbowe, Brian Hand, and M. L. Legg. 2001. "Using the Science Writing Heuristic to Move Toward an Inquiry-Based Laboratory Curriculum: An example From Physical Equilibrium." *Journal of Chemical Education* 78: 1680–686.

Wallace, Carolyn, Brian Hand, and Vaughn Prain. 2004. *Writing and Learning in the Science Classroom*. Kluwer Press: Boston.

Wallace, Carolyn, Brian Hand, and Eun-Mi Yang. 2004. "The Science Writing Heuristic: Using Writing as a Tool for Learning in the Laboratory." In E. Wendy Saul, ed. *Border Crossing: Essays on Literacy and Science*. Newark, DE: International Reading Association.

# Have A Go! Appendix Overview

Getting started with a new approach can be a daunting task. One of the suggestions that emerged when teachers read the first draft of this text was: Can you break it up into some small, easy steps to help us get started? These appendixes are our response with a resounding, "Yes!" As you work through each of the chapters, we have encouraged you in different places in the text to "have a go!" and find your way to these small challenges in the back of the book.

Appendix A: The Start of Your Journey

Appendix B: Your Teacher Voice

Appendix C: Aligning Learning and Teaching

Appendix D: Negotiating Your Own Meaning

Appendix E: Examining Conceptual Frameworks

Appendix F: Management vs. Teaching

Appendix G: Custom Professional Development Program Design

Appendix H: What Do You and Your Students Think About Teaching and Learning?

Appendix I: Student Questions

Appendix J: Using Questions to Guide Discussion

Appendix K: Making Claims, Providing Evidence

Appendix L: Assessing Student Writing

# The Start of Your Journey

Are you a good teacher? Do you have nagging doubts about certain aspects of your teaching, student learning, and how to get your students engaged? Take the time to complete the following list of questions to start your process of working through this book.

1. What is a good teacher?

2. Are you a good teacher, based on your answer to Question 1? What is the basis of your ideas of what is a good teacher?

3. What kind of engagement do your students have during your lessons?

4. How do you evaluate yourself professionally, that is, what list of criteria do you use to measure your teaching?

5. How do you decide what is taught during a unit and plan lessons?

6. What are the most important factors for student learning in your classroom?

7. How do you know if your students have learned what you are teaching?

Were these questions easy to answer? When was the last time you thought about these questions? Are these the issues that you discuss with your colleagues and in your staff meetings? Teacher professional development often doesn't engage you any better than we often engage our students. To examine these questions, we encourage you to actively investigate your teaching to really get at these issues.

Keep these questions and answers handy as you work through the book. Spend time talking with your colleagues about these questions and their answers. You may find that you are so busy with the details of your work that you aren't spending enough time thinking about the big picture. Working through the SWH approach will push your thinking and will add depth to your understanding of what happens in your classroom related to your teaching and students' learning. The "Have a Go!" exercises will help you focus on these issues, so take time to explore them. This can serve as a learning journal or ongoing personal assessment. They can be great dialogue starters as well.

# Your Teacher Voice

## Teacher's Voice

After a twenty-five-year career as a high school science teacher, I was pretty much set in my ways of disseminating information to my students. We would have lecture/note taking, discussion, lab investigations, worksheets, cooperative learning groups, projects, and so on. It was not a bad classroom in my opinion. The classroom was very organized. The activities were varied. I was trying to include all students by doing a variety of activities and using a variety of methods that would incorporate the different learning styles of students.

The teacher's voice here can describe many in the profession. Consider your personal answers to these questions:

❖ How can I invigorate my classroom?

❖ How can I get more students involved in their learning?

❖ How can I do all this and still have my students improve their test scores?

❖ How can I make my teaching more stimulating and intellectually engaging for myself?

Depending where you are in your career the answers may vary, but it is safe to assume that if you are taking the time to explore the SWH process that you are still looking for answers for how to become a better teacher.

Many beginning teachers are overwhelmed with procedures, classroom management, and what to teach, while the experienced teachers are often nagged by questions related to lack of student interest and achievement, which can cause self-doubt and adds to the number of teachers that leave the classroom each year.

Now write your own paragraph that describes where you are right now in your career. Put it all in there—successes, failures, doubts, frustrations, and persisting questions.

After completing your paragraph, go back and read it. Share it with a colleague. What are the common themes that run through your writing? Now list just what you are looking for in your professional growth using the four questions listed earlier as your guide. Keep these questions and your paragraph so you can review them after each chapter and evaluate your own professional growth. If you do consider yourself a good teacher, why do the nagging doubts persist? Use this book as a tool to better understand what you do as a teacher and how this affects the learning of your students.

# Aligning Learning and Teaching

We are all learning every day. Do you think about how you learn and what support or structure you prefer when you learn? "Lifelong learners" is a tired cliché. Everyone learns until they die. Our job as teachers requires us to think more deeply about learning and understand how we learn and how our students learn.

Think about something that you have chosen to learn lately: a new skill, a hobby, or perhaps a language. What conditions did you prefer for your learning—not as teachers but as adults learning something new? Try completing the following task:

1. Write down something that you would consider yourself an expert at.

2. Next write down something you are terrible at, in other words, something you don't do well at all.

3. Return to where your expert task is written and write down the five ways you became an expert at this task, skill, or the like.

See if your answers match these common responses:

❖ Have time to explore on my own

❖ Given opportunities to ask experts

❖ Have the right equipment available to use

❖ Have interest in the topic

❖ Provided opportunities to practice

❖ Controlled the pace of learning

These responses seem to be straightforward and reasonable. Now go to the flip side—make a short list of why you struggle so much with the task that you don't do well at all. Many times, the responses are:

❖ Don't have interest in learning

❖ Was told exactly what to do or forced to do it

❖ Have no skill at doing it

❖ Answer questions out of the text or rote learning

❖ Take the experts' ideas or strategies word for word or step by step

Now ask your students to complete the same exercise. You may want to tell them that you are reading a book that focuses on teaching and learning and are trying to learn more about these two concepts. Talk through their answers and share your answers with them. How do the two lists compare? Do your students have similar answers to your own?

The question is, "Why do we not put the learning strategies that are most effective for ourselves as learners into our classrooms?" Of course, one of the first responses to that question is, "Yeah, but we have to . . . " Here are two interesting points to ponder:

❖ First, why is it that when someone talks to a group of people, or shows a group of people a new skill, that no two people in the group repeat the message or skill in exactly the same manner as the person who was in charge?

❖ Second, why is it that all students are not succeeding equally well if the current strategies implemented mean that as teachers we control the information they receive?

Understanding teaching and learning is fundamental to teaching with Questions, Claims, and Evidence. Continue to reflect back on this exercise as you implement the SWH approach in the classroom.

# Negotiating Your Own Meaning

After reading the learning section in Chapter 2, spend time thinking about what we told you about learning and what you already know about meaning making. Your goal with negotiation is to better connect all the concepts about learning together in a sensible manner leading to a better understanding on your part.

Then have a colleague, friend, student, or someone else read the section. Ask them to then negotiate their meaning. After they have finished with their personal negotiation, explain learning based on your negotiated meaning. Encourage your partner to ask questions, challenge your thinking, and interact on the ideas of learning. Then reverse roles.

Answer these questions after completing the task:

1. How did you process the reading to make connections with your prior understanding of learning?

2. How did your negotiation of meaning process take place? Did you dialogue with yourself, make notes, draw diagrams, or something else?

3. How did your discussion or public negotiation affect your ideas? Did you have to shift or did the ideas come into sharper focus?

4. How would you describe what is happening with this exercise in terms of learning?

# Examining Conceptual Frameworks

Before beginning a unit you need to have a solid understanding of your conceptual framework of the topic. Have a go at building a representation of that framework. The starting point is what understanding of the topic you want your students to leave the classroom with at the conclusion of the unit. These should be the big ideas and should be the focus of a unit. Too often as content specialists we get caught up in the facts and confuse all the facts around a topic, never revealing or examining the big ideas with our students. Work through this process to begin to focus on conceptual frameworks. The process will be revisited later on in the book.

1. Put the topic in the box.

2. What are the big ideas? List them in the circles.

3. Take all the ideas of your topic and add them in smaller circles around the big ideas.

4. Draw lines to show how they connect and use linking words on the lines to show how the two connected pieces relate.

Now compare your map with the textbook or other resources you may use for this topic. How does your understanding align with these sources? An example of one teacher's concept map can be found in Figure E.2.

# SWH Tool

**Figure E.1.** *Blank Concept Map*

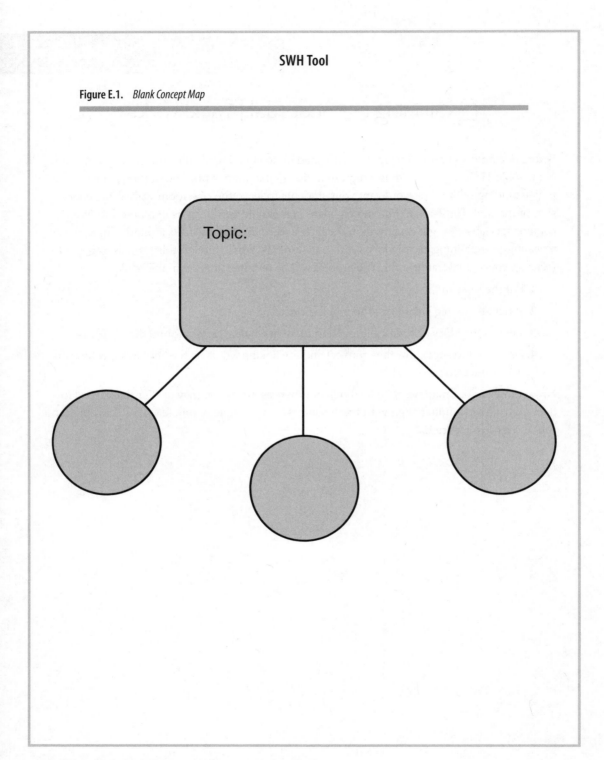

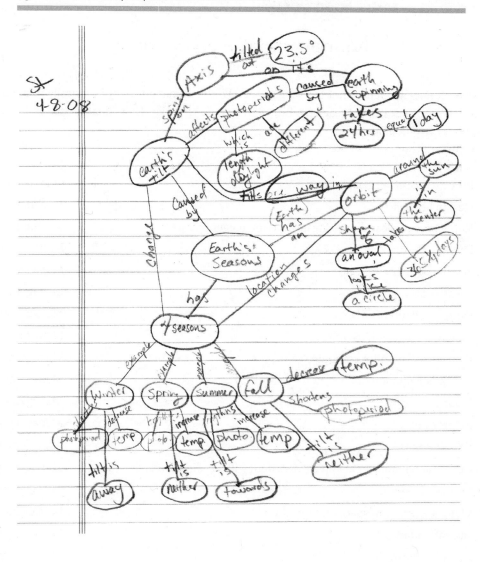

# Management vs. Teaching

Classroom management is not teaching. Good classroom management is critically important for a classroom, but it is not teaching. List all that you do in a day. Then identify each task as either teaching or management.

Compare your list with the following:

| | |
|---|---|
| Provide access to books/print | Management |
| Design lessons | Teaching |
| Know how the learning today fits into the bigger picture | Teaching |
| Provide resources | Management |
| Set up cooperative groups | Management |
| Create learning centers | Management |
| Design bulletin boards | Management |
| Manage space for kids to work | Management |
| Provide and monitor computer access | Management |
| Set up lab equipment | Management |
| Manage time | Management |
| Enforce procedures/rules | Management |
| Scheduling | Management |
| Collect and manage data on each student (IEP, reading levels) | Management |
| Provide textbooks | Management |
| Manage classroom space and furniture | Management |
| Take attendance | Management |
| Complete forms | Management |
| Ask probing questions | Teaching |
| Evaluate student learning | Teaching |

If you look at the list and disagree or are shocked, review the discussion of what is teaching and what is learning in Chapters 2 and 3. How does your list compare to the list above? What are you investing most of your time, effort, and focus on—management or teaching? Don't misunderstand the point of this activity. Management is necessary, but teaching and learning should be at the center of what we do in the classroom.

# Custom Professional Development Program Design

Let's start with describing your typical professional development session.

**1.** List all the components of the session/sessions.

**2.** Go through the description and underline all the components that you found helpful in your professional growth.

**3.** What do you think is missing?

**4.** Make a list of what you would want in a professional development program that you can customize for yourself.

Does your list include:

❖ Freedom to dig into issues and ideas and time to process them?

❖ Choice in direction and pace?

❖ How you want to learn?

❖ Choice in mentors/experts?

❖ A long-term strategy that isn't pressured by need for right-now results?

❖ More?

Use this process to help you design the professional development process for your own study of the SWH approach. Design a process that matches what you believe about learning and what you know about yourself. Set up the parameters that will help you succeed. Teachers who read early drafts of this book set up a variety of structures that helped them create active learning experiences around this book, including a regular professional book club with members who read and discussed parts of the book systematically. Another group created an online discussion board where they regularly posted about what they were attempting in the classroom, frustrations, successes, and questions for response from others. Another group set up opportunities to visit each other's classrooms for observation and team teaching, particularly when they were working through helping their students with Questions, Claims, Evidence, and Argumentation. Look at your list and think about what constitutes solid professional development for you and then put those structures into place as you actively investigate science inquiry, language practices, and teaching in the service of learning.

# What Do You and Your Students Think About Teaching and Learning?

Take some time and answer the following questions and ask your students to answer them as well:

- ❖ What is learning?
- ❖ What is teaching?
- ❖ How do you like to learn?
- ❖ How do you like to teach?
- ❖ How do the answers compare?

You may find the answers that you and your students give to these questions are quite interesting. In responding to these questions, some students can be quite insightful into teaching and learning. Others will be skilled at describing the traditional models they have experienced.

Have your ideas shifted from your work in Section I? What changes are occurring? Go back periodically and answer the questions again to serve as a gauge of your construction of knowledge related to teaching and learning.

This experience provides a perfect opportunity to practice classroom negotiation skills (see Chapter 7)—both for you and your students. After students have had a chance to respond to the two questions about learning and teaching described above, get the class to break into small groups and share their answers to the question: How do you learn something you want to learn outside of school such as a hobby or knowledge of personal interest?

Have students compare their answers to this question with their responses to the earlier questions about what is learning and teaching. Don't interfere with the process by imposing your own answers. Ask them where they find similarities and, more likely, where they find differences. After they discuss their ideas in small groups, give the entire group the task of working together to identify what an ideal learning situation should be. Stay out of the discussion but use your teaching skills to move them forward. If the students are trapped in a "school mind-set" of trying to guess what the teacher wants for an answer, you may need to prompt with more questions or ask other students to respond to ideas being presented. For example, if a student won't engage in the process and is concerned about his or her ideas not being "right," you may ask, "What do you think about what Susie said?" after she gave an answer.

This experience will help students practice negotiating their ideas in a group and will also start to move the classroom dynamic from teacher control of discourse to a climate of public negotiation of meaning and need to defend and challenge ideas that are presented. This is a critical classroom skill for both you and your students. Classroom discourse and the negotiation of ideas are critical to the successful implementation of the SWH approach.

You might be wondering how this "have a go" exercise is different from what you experienced in Appendix C. In the previous engagement, we asked you and your students to reveal your personal learning style and preferences. In this exercise, we are asking the group to negotiate a common understanding. This experience gives you practice in helping students not only negotiate a group understanding but also engage in the art of argumentation, which is at the heart of the SWH approach and the work of scientists. As an added benefit, the students will reveal to you their thoughts about teaching and learning—they will reveal their learning histories, what has made learning difficult for them as well as easy, and they will soon see that what might have been a negative learning experience for one, was a very positive experience for the peer sitting across the table. Your role is to sit back and get out of the way . . . engage in the art of listening and how to get them to listen and respond to each other.

## From the Students

In this example, the students in one class had a group discussion and generated a concept map about the work of a scientist. This could be another option for this "Have a Go" exercise.

**Figure H.1.** *Student-generated concept map about scientists*

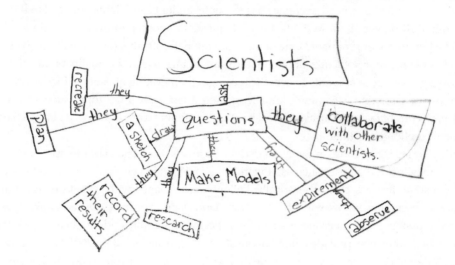

# Student Questions

People are naturally curious and want to find out the "why" of what they experience. Why don't we see that in school? Curiosity is a human characteristic that isn't always expressed in class to the level we would like or need to create spaces where students are highly engaged in the subject matter. Why do you think students don't ask questions spontaneously and continuously as they did when they were younger? One of the foundational shifts that occurs with the SWH approach is a reemergence of a questioning nature and an increase in the quality of questions.

Have a go with your students to see if you can get them asking questions. Pick a topic unrelated to your class that is common knowledge and is currently a hot topic, such as a sports controversy, current event, or local issue. Pick a nonthreatening topic that doesn't bring charged emotional reactions into the mix.

With your students bring up the issue in casual conversation. Then start to ask some questions that may include phrases such as, "I wonder . . .", "Why do you think . . .", or other open-ended question. Just ask them rhetorically. Follow your musings with "What do you think?" After some discussion follow with the question "Don't you ever have questions like these?" Begin a discussion about their questions. If the process can get the students' heads to shift out of school mode they may provide a flood of questions. A critical goal of the SWH approach is to get the students to shift out of school mode and back into their curiosity mode and begin asking "why" questions once again.

# Using Questions to Guide Discussion

Have a go at using questions to move and guide a classroom discussion toward your curricular goals. Questioning as a teacher in the SWH approach is a critical teaching skill. In this Have a Go! just take some time to play around with questioning.

Select a topic and specific learning experience that you would like to use with your class. In the text of Chapter 6 the topic was forces and motion and the learning experience for the SWH was building and launching paper rockets.

When you have your topic ask your student to generate ideas and what they know about the topic on sticky notes. Then have them put the sticky notes on a board. Assess the notes and look for any notes that are aligned with your goals. Then use questions to move those ideas to the center of the class focus.

The discussion could like this:

TEACHER: Looking at your notes I wonder if we can group these ideas. Can you see any categories or groups that apply? Can you organize the notes by your categories?

The focus of the notes can align with your goals for the unit. Use a conversation to lead the group to focus on these notes. Be sure to avoid being controlling. Get students to ask key questions. For example, if the group has a sticky note that matches your goals, quietly suggest a question to the student or students who wrote the goal to ask the class. Follow with a question, "What do you think about that?" Direct this question to the students who designed the question originally. As you progress, the students will need less prompting as they take ownership in process and realize that they are partners in guiding the learning.

# From the Students

**Figure J.1.**  *An Example of a Group-Negotiated Questioning Board*

# Making Claims, Providing Evidence

Read the following mystery story and then develop claims and evidence that explains the mystery.

### The Mr. Xavier Mystery

You and your partner are private detectives who have been hired to investigate the death of the wealthy but eccentric Mr. Xavier, a man who was well known for his riches and his reclusive nature. He avoided being around others because he was always filled with anxiety and startled easily. He also suffered from paranoia, and he would fire servants who he had employed for a long time because he feared they were secretly plotting against him. He would also eat the same meal for dinner every night: two steaks cooked rare and two baked potatoes with sour cream. Upon arriving at the tragic scene, you are told that Mr. Xavier was found dead in his home early this morning by the servants. The previous evening after the chef had prepared the usual dinner for Mr. Xavier, the servants had been dismissed early in order to avoid returning home during last night's terrible storm. When they returned in the morning, Mr. Xavier's body was found facedown in the dining room. Looking into the room, you start your investigation. The large window in the dining room has been shattered and appears to have been smashed open from the outside. The body exhibits laceration wounds and lies facedown by the table, and there is a large red stain on the carpet that emanates from under the body. An open bottle of red wine and a partially eaten steak still remain on the table. A chair that has been tipped over is next to the body, and under the table is a knife with blood on it.

After reading the story ask students to make a claim about what happened to Mr. Xavier. Ask them to list all the data provided (let them decide on how to represent this data) and then write their explanation of the event. Using different group strategies, work to a whole-group discussion of what happened. Encourage students to ask questions. Target students who have differing claims to challenge their peers about the differences. Quietly and privately ask a student who has differing ideas what he or she thinks of another explanation and then prompt him or her to ask questions to challenge the differences. This is a powerful exercise to promote understanding of evidence through practice as well as a fun and engaging practice of social negotiation and argumentation. As discussion moves along statements will range from statement of direct data from the story to interjection of opinion. The beauty of this exercise is that it is open-ended as you aren't given enough information to arrive at a definitive answer, just like many real investigations that your students will pursue. Watch for opinion to creep in and prompt challenging of opinion as contrasted to data. See an example of a student's SWH process in relation to the *Mr. Xavier Mystery* in Figure K.1.

# From the Students

**Figure K.1.**  *Fifth-grade Student Provides Claims and Evidence About What Happened to Mr. Xavier*

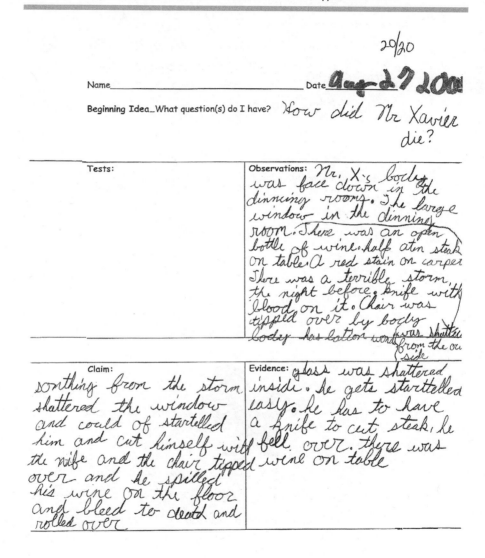

20/20

Name _____  Date Aug 27 200

Beginning Idea...What question(s) do I have?  How did Mr Xavier die?

Tests:

Observations: Mr. X's body was face down in the dinning room. The large window in the dinning room. There was an open bottle of wine. half atin steak on table. A red stain on carpet. There was a terrible storm the night before. knife with blood on it. Chair was tipped over by body body has lotion word was shuttu was shutter from the ou side

Claim:
sonthing from the storm shattered the window and could of startelled him and cut hinself with the nife and the chair tipped over and he spilled his wine on the floor and bleed to death and rolled over

Evidence: glass was shattered inside. he gets starttelled easly. he has to have a knife to cut steak. he fell over. there was wine on table

*continues on next page*

**How do my ideas compare with others?** Other people had good Idea's. Most people thought the chef. Or the storm did it. Everyone looked very closely. It was very fun and intereresting

**How have my ideas changed?** ~I need more information.

Check for finger prints on knife. Otopsey. test the stain. Question chef

# Assessing Student Writing

Assessing our students' writing is always a challenge. Should we focus on the mechanics of writing: correct spelling, punctuation, organization, and flow? Or, should we be more concerned with their creativity, voice, word choice, and the ideas and content presented? Of course, we want to reveal their understanding of the science content we are working with through any given unit. Have they grasped the big ideas? How are the students able to show their developing conceptual understanding through the written word?

Throughout this book, we share many assessment tools with you that have been used and developed in classrooms. Yet, in this Have a Go! experience, we would like to explore your thoughts and values when it comes to good writing.

First, begin by flipping back through this book and taking a look at each writing sample. What grade would you give each student writer? Why? Do you immediately see the misspelled words and convention issues and instantly decide on a lower grade? Are you able to look beyond that and see the content the student is wrestling with in relation to the big idea? How is the student able to negotiate the language of science with the creative writing opportunities being presented by the teacher?

Second, take a stack of your own student papers. Read them and sort them into approximately three piles: excellent, good, needs support. Now take a careful look at each stack. What are the characteristics or features that you see consistent in each of the piles of papers? You now have a developing rubric to share with your students. This exercise also reveals to you what you value in your students' writing and puts you in a position to then help them to become better writers of science.

# References

Ausubel, David P. 1968. *Educational Psychology: A Cognitive View*. New York: Holt, Rinehart and Winston.

Bazerman, Charles. 2008. *Handbook of Research on Writing: History, Society, School, Individual, Text*. New York: Lawrence Erlbaum Associates.

Bereiter, Carl, and Marlene Scardamalia. 1987. *The Psychology of Written Communication*. Hillsdale, NJ: Erlbaum and Associates.

Billmeyer, Rachel. 2004. *Strategic Reading in the Content Areas: Practical Applications for Creating a Thinking Environment*. Omaha, NE: Rachel & Associates.

Cazden, Courtney B. 2001. *Classroom Discourse: The Language of Teaching and Learning*. 2nd ed. Portsmouth, NH: Heinemann.

Ford, Michael. 2008. "Disciplinary Authority and Accountability in Scientific Practice and Learning." *Science Education* 92: 404–23.

Galbraith, David. 1999. "Writing as a Knowledge-Constituting Process." In Mark Torrance and David Galbraith, eds. *Knowing What to Write: Conceptual Processes in Text Production*, 139–59. Amsterdam: Amsterdam University Press.

Gee, James P. 1996. *Social Linguistics and Literacies: Ideology in Discourses*. 2nd ed. Philadelphia: Routledge/Farmer.

Gowin, Dixie. 1981. *Educating*. Ithaca, NY: Cornell University Press.

Halliday, Michael A. K. 1975. *Learning How to Mean*. London: Arnold Press.

Hand, Brian, and Carolyn Keys. 1999. "Inquiry Investigation." *The Science Teacher* 66(4): 27–29.

Hand, Brian, Liesl Hohenshell, and Vaughn Prain. 2004. "Exploring Students' Responses to Conceptual Questions When Engaged with Planned Writing Experiences: A Study with Year 10 Science Students." *Journal of Research in Science Teaching* 41(2): 186–210.

Klein, Perry D. 1999. "Reopening Inquiry into Cognitive Processes in Writing-to-Learn." *Educational Psychology Review* 11(3): 203–70.

Lemke, Jay. 1990. *Talking Science: Language, Learning, and Values*. Norwood, NJ: Ablex.

Llewellyn, Douglas. 2001. *Inquire Within: Implementing Inquiry-Based Science Standards*. Thousand Oaks, CA: Sage Publications.

Marzano, Robert J., Barbara B. Gaddy, and Ceri Dean. 2000. *What Works in Classroom Instruction*. Aurora, CO: Mid-continent Research for Education and Learning.

National Research Council. 1996. *National Science Education Standards*. Washington, DC: National Academy Press.

Norris, Steven P., and Linda M. Phillips. 2003. "How Literacy in Its Fundamental Sense Is Central to Scientific Literacy." *Science Education* 87: 224–40.

Piaget, Jean, and Barbel Inhelder. 1969. *The Psychology of the Child*. New York: Basic Books.

Pinnell, Gay Su. 1985. "Ways to Look at the Functions of Children's Language." In A. Jaggar and M. T. Smith-Burke, eds. *Observing the Language Learner*: 57–72. Newark, DE: International Reading Association.

Rivard, Leonard P., and Stanley B. Straw. 2000. "The Effect of Talk and Writing on Learning Science: An Exploratory Study." *Science Education* 84(5): 566–93.

Saul, E. Wendy. 2004. *Border Crossing: Essays on Literacy and Science*. Newark, DE: International Reading Association/National Science Teachers Association.

Smith, Frank. 1977. "The Uses of Language." *Language Arts* 54(6): 638–44.

Strike, Kenneth A. 1987. "Toward a Coherent Constructivism." In J. Novak, ed. Vol. I of *Proceedings of the 2nd Int. Seminar Misconceptions and Educational Strategies in Science and Mathematics*, 481–89. Ithaca, NY: Cornell University.

Vygotsky, Lev. 1978. *The Mind in Society*. Cambridge, MA: Harvard University Press.

# Index